DO YOURSELF A FLAVOUR

DO YOURSELF A FLAVOUR

75 EASY RECIPES TO FEED **YOURSELF**, YOUR **FLATMATES** AND YOUR **FREEZER**

FLISS FREEBORN

EBURY
PRESS

5 THINGS, 5 WAYS

CONTENTS

The photograph on the front cover is the Red Pesto and Aubergine Pasta on page 58

THE WARMEST OF WELCOMES

Hello, lovelies.

Thanks ever so much for picking up this cookbook. While it's tempting to make this introduction all about me, that would be self-indulgent and unhelpful, so let's make it all about you instead.

I'm guessing that you're a young(ish) person on a relatively sensible budget who can chop an onion – and possibly make a passable Bolognese when threatened – but you might gravitate towards pesto-pasta or beans on toast for dinner when left to your own devices.

If the above sounds perfect to you, and you're already delighted with how you cook and eat, then congratulations – you've just got yourself a brand-new laptop stand. No shade, by the way. Some folks are definitely in the 'food-is-fuel' camp, and that's absolutely fine. Just nod feverishly and tell your aunty what a brilliant cookbook it is.

But with any luck, you'll want to use this book for its intended purpose: to take your cooking up a notch while still clinging to a modest food budget. Oh, and to really start enjoying yourself in the kitchen, too.

Here you'll find some din-spiration that doesn't involve a riot of expensive or completely bizarre ingredients, utilises the culinary skills you already have, and doesn't require you to buy any more equipment for your (probably) shared, cramped kitchen. I imagine you'll want dinners that punch above their weight for the effort and ingredients involved, because, well, who on earth wouldn't?

I'm also going to make the bold assumption that you have some friends you enjoy spending time with, who like you enough to let you cook them dinner now and again. Said friends, however, might arrive with an erratic spattering of dietary requirements that inevitably put pressure on the host, all too often forcing the gastronomically ostracised to bring their own food in a sad little Tupperware.

Well, it's time to banish sad little Tupperwares, and do yourself a flavour. Because *as luck would have it*, this book responds to all of the above challenges in a way that I hope is readable, understandable and useful. The bits that are not useful, understandable or readable, I hope at least border on humorous. If that's not your bag, you'll have to forgive me for playing with recipe formatting for the sake of a cheap laugh every now and again.

In this wodge of former tree you're holding, there are 75 recipes, all of which I use on a regular basis in my own kitchen – and in other people's when I inevitably end up staying and cooking dinner for everyone. The sort of food I make adapts according to where I am and who I'm with, so rather than swinging on the classic trope of 'breakfast, lunch, dinner, desserts, snacks', or even categorising by ingredient, the chapters are organised in a way that reflects the life experiences of being a skint-ish member of The Yoof.

These recipes should work for you whether you're at uni, graduated, working a customer service job, doing the nine-to-five or simply hiding under a duvet avoiding hustle culture and questions about your 'career'.[1]

So go forth, make a huge mess and have loads of fun – or go fifth and do it all neatly and perfectly without treading bits of red onion skin into your bedroom carpet after cooking yourself and your ravenous flatmate a lovely dinner.

Have fun, folks.

Love,

Fliss x

PS If it all goes tits-up, I've written a common troubleshooting FAQ (Frequently Arsed-up Quandaries), which you'll find on pages 178–81.

PPS Oh, me? You want to know about me? Well, I've been cooking for ten years – since the age of 14. Then, when I got to uni, I started a food blog. And now I've written a book, which, by some order of miracles, you're now reading. There's more to the story than this, obviously, but I did say I'd try not to make this all about me, so that's your lot for a hot minute.

[1] Solidarity, my friend.

HOW TO ABUSE THIS BOOK

Make a cup of tea now, because here is some very important information for you to read before you decide to cook one of these recipes.

PORTION SIZES

The majority of my recipes are designed for two: either to be split between you and a loved one or, if you're cooking for just yourself, for you to have the other portion for lunch the next day. Absolutely feel free to halve the quantities if you don't want lunch, or double them if you're feeding flatmates or families. Just be aware that two is default rather than one, because it's easier to use a whole tin of tomatoes, or a whole packet of parsley, rather than using just what you need and then having the rest fester in the fridge all week, unused. Chapter 4: Feed Your Friends (or Your Freezer) and Chapter 5: Low and Slow, Bro both have slightly larger portion sizes and should give you plenty of batch-cooking options if that's more your jam.

Portion-wise, it's probably useful to bear in mind that I feed some very hungry caterpillars on a regular basis, so if you're a smaller human who doesn't need to inhale a gargantuan amount of calories at the end of the day lest you faint, then my recipes will probably give you a little more than you need. You can, of course, adjust the quantities to suit your appetite, but don't be afraid to make slightly more: there's always Frankenstein Fries (page 79) to use up any of those annoyingly small grubbules of leftover meals that take up all the Gü ramekins and clutter the fridge, plus loads of other ideas for using up leftover ingredients scattered through the book.

Please don't ever throw edible stuff away, by the way. You'll soon see that food waste is one of my pet peeves, and should be one of yours, too. There are loads of handy food-waste tips throughout.

TIMINGS

What takes me five minutes could take you ten if you don't yet know your way round a butternut squash, or if you have to climb on a chair to reach the spices in the top cupboard (do move them to somewhere more accessible). Everyone is different: some of my capillaries nearly burst when I witnessed a friend take seven minutes to peel one potato, but equally I will watch in awe as my cheffier friends dice a carrot in the time it takes me to sneeze. It's pretty obvious to me that how long a recipe might take is a piece-of-string question, so all timings in this book are rough estimates only.

I'd also like to encourage you to see your time in the kitchen as less of a chore. While there are shortcuts and cheats and hacks you can use (and this book is full of them), it's not all about being in, out and shaking it all about in 30 seconds with two ingredients, as TikTok would lead you to believe. Some stuff, you'll be displeased to hear, actually takes *time*. Including cooking onions. No one in the history of mankind has fully cooked an onion in 3–4 minutes. They just haven't. It's all a massive lie made up by Big Onion to make you buy more onions under the assumption that they're quick to cook.

MEASURING QUANTITIES

I cook everything by feel, using the distant voices of the nonnas I never had. Who knows how much roux I'll end up with? Not me, that's for sure. Not Nonna, either.

I'm so gung-ho in this regard that I even judge bread ingredients by eye because I like to live dangerously. I understand, however, that when writing recipes for others, this is extraordinarily impractical. To this end, all quantities are presented in tablespoons, teaspoons, mugs, cups, tins and packets, plus grams where it's appropriate – but I'll never use grams alone for savoury recipes, so breathe if you're worried about not having scales. For baking, I do have a set of digital scales that I use lots of the time, but you can make the majority of the sweet recipes without them, including – gasp – a whole sponge cake (see page 172).

For reference, a tablespoon is roughly 15ml, a teaspoon is 5ml, and no, it doesn't matter if you don't have quite enough or a bit too much of X, Y and Z for the most part. If I say to use a tin of something, I mean a standard-sized tin, most often 400g/400ml. When I say mug, I mean one of those standard ones you get for free at careers fairs rather than anything bigger or smaller – roughly 300ml, but again, precision isn't too important. A handful is around half a mug, in case you're wondering. I know this is all like learning a new language if you're not used to it, but it'll become intuitive eventually. You'll see as we get into it that I'll encourage you to nurture, then trust your instincts as you go.

To that end, you'll probably notice that my style of instructional writing is quite detailed. This is because I want you to understand exactly *why* you're doing something, not just how. Don't be put off by the large chunks of text – this doesn't mean that the recipe is complicated in any way; there are probably just a few important signs that I want you to be looking out for that other recipe books might omit for the sake of a nicer-looking page layout. I'll always choose clarity over brevity, as *I* want the recipes to succeed just as much as *you* want the recipes to succeed. In fact, I've written a whole troubleshooting guide to refer back to (see pages 178–81), just in case things do go wrong at any point.

DIETARIES

I'll throw my hands up here now and admit that I happily eat anything that once farted, swam, or squawked, but I recognise that the societal need to eat less meat outweighs my love of scraping marrow out of bones with a chopstick at the end of a meal. This is reflected by the fact that 61 out of the 75 recipes in this book are either vegan, vegetarian or can be made without meat to no detrimental effect. It's a happy circumstance that my love of umami flavours has driven me to create recipes that have the same depth of flavour without any animals on the advisory board.

There's also a selection of gluten-free options for those whose microvilli are plotting against them, and a good number of dairy-free recipes, too, if lactose poses a gut-rumbling risk. This inclusivity is to do with my unwavering rule at any Food-based Gathering I host: everyone must be able to eat the same main dish. This sometimes means doing a long think (usually in a lecture, or at work) about recipes and ingredients, but I'll cover more of that in my brief interlude about how to cook happily for others on pages 98–9.

My one other thing to say here is that I tend to avoid meat substitutes, preferring to use mushrooms and lentils where needed. You can, of course, do as you please, so do feel free to use any plant-based substitutes, including for dairy, where you like.

For reference, the dietary symbols you'll see in this book are as follows:

GF = Gluten-free

DF = Dairy-free

V = Vegetarian

VG = Vegan

I'll add an O when the recipe can easily be adapted to each requirement with substitutions or ingredient choices, i.e. GFO = Gluten-free Option

EVERYTHING YOU NEED (OR DON'T)

INGREDIENTS AND COSTS

The recipes in this book make use of a large range of inexpensive ingredients widely available in the UK. I've made sure that 99 per cent of the ingredients required in this book can be found in any Lidl or Aldi, so by default, any of the Big Four. The ingredients that are not stocked in my beloved Mid-Sized-German Supermarkets (yet) are also the fanciest in this book: tahini, bulgur wheat and harissa paste. Happily, these are all readily available elsewhere, both in larger British supermarkets and your local Middle Eastern shop, which you should definitely visit for cheaper spices and herbs – and an array of other exciting things – if you have one nearby.

While this isn't *wholly* a budget cookbook, if an ingredient does cost more – for example, a wedge of Parmesan, a bottle of red wine or some olive oil – then it should last you several, if not plenty, of meals. There should be a chance to use 'pricier' stuff (including what I call 'detail' ingredients, such as fresh herbs, olives, capers and chillies) a good few times throughout the book, and I've signposted where they are in the footnotes, so you shouldn't be left with jars or packets of open stuff lying about too often.

Additionally, recipes can always be made cheaper by replacing certain ingredients with others, and where possible, I'll do a budget-swap option if the original has one or two slightly more expensive components. On that note, I've never been the biggest fan of doing per-serve costings, because it doesn't take into account the fact that you spent 89p on a jar of cinnamon only to use 0.2g of the stuff, or found a whole leg of lamb for £3.89 in the supermarket reduced chiller (which I highly recommend you make use of, by the way), so you won't see exact costings next to each recipe. I'll just indicate in the preamble if there's anything more expensive you need to watch for, or if the recipe is particularly easy on the old bank account.

UNSTAPLE YOUR STORE CUPBOARD

Anyone that's been within six feet of my personal life will know that I have never been one for order, rules or lists, so cookbooks that tell me to stock my cupboard with a different vinegar for every mood and discuss at length the importance of my olive oil's virginity have always tickled my irk-biscuit.

Everyone likes to eat different things, everyone has a different budget, everyone has a different-sized cupboard, and really, the only things I can think of that occur with tedious regularity within this book are tinned tomatoes, salt, black pepper, lemon juice, wine and cooking oil (either light olive oil or vegetable oil; in most cases, it won't matter).

Therefore, I'm not going to order you to go and stock up on the finest herbs, spices, stock cubes and whatnot, especially as you probably have your own eclectic selection already. There is no essential ingredient list for this cookbook either, but a quick lick through the index will give you an overall flavour of what sort of things are going in your dinner if you're more of a list person and would like to feel a little more prepared.

THAT SAID, LET'S HAVE A QUICK RAZZ AROUND SALT AND OIL

The first thing that transformed my cooking was learning to use salt properly. The second thing that transformed my cooking was no longer being afraid of fat. If you can get your head around using these two elements more liberally, then seriously, you're in for a treat: so grow your glugs, and puff up those pinches. My recommended reading on this is *Salt, Fat, Acid, Heat* by Samin Nosrat, which is a gem of a book if you're properly interested in food, and bears the credit for my deepened understanding of the scientific principles involved in much of my cooking.

An important note for this book is that I rarely quantify the amount of salt (or fat) you'll need, and when I do, it's an approximation than a hard-and-fast rule. This is partially because a teaspoon of one brand of salt will taste different to a teaspoon of another brand, and partially because I want you to learn to know what tastes good to you. So when I instruct you to 'season to taste' or even just 'season', I do mean for you to use your mouth. Not tasting your food as you go is like trying to drive a car with your eyes wide shut; everything that goes into the pan should be sampled regularly, using a teaspoon that you wash each time (that's if you're cooking for someone other than your lover, who, all things considered, probably shouldn't care). Tasting will enable you to decide the level of salinity or acidity you're after, and after a while, you'll learn what a dish needs without having to think about it consciously. Your senses are arguably far more important than what any timer or scale has to say on the matter, so listen to them all – sight, sound, touch, as well as taste and smell.

EQUIPMENT, OR LACK THEREOF

To cook decent meals, you really don't need much. Like I said earlier, I hate lists, so I'm never going to write you a prescription for kitchen equipment. Chances are, if you're an adult who's ever cobbled together a pasta bake, you'll probably have everything you need already.

I'll outline what equipment you'll be needing within the recipe's context, but if you don't have a square baking tin, or a serving plate, or a round cake tin, then chill. It's gucci. Use what you have – chances are it'll work and you'll have a good time. If you really feel yourself reaching for something that's not there on more than a few occasions, go and root around in your local charity shop or search for it on eBay for it before getting into bed with that ethically questionable website that we all know and really shouldn't love.

And just for some reassurance, here's a long list of things I don't own, and you don't need to own either: a stand mixer, a hand mixer, a jug blender, a spiraliser, an apple corer, a proper fish slice that's not completely melted at one end, a nutcracker, a blowtorch, an egg timer, an egg maker, an oven thermometer, a meat thermometer, cookie cutters, a cardboard cut-out of Michael Palin, a Le Creuset casserole dish, an enamel pie tin, a wok, a tofu press, an apron, a meat cleaver... and, until very recently, a pastry brush. I used to just use kitchen roll to dab egg over things willy-nilly. My point is, you can cope just fine without loads of this stuff, and if you already have it, then brilliant. Use it to your advantage.

There are, however, two gadgety items I own that are both very useful. The first is a stick blender, which for £9.99 not only obliterates formerly chunky soup down to the smoothest of purées, but also smushes curry paste ingredients together, whips cream or egg whites if the balloon-whisk-and-triceps combo is off sick, and makes very, very smooth and frothy hot chocolate, which you can find on page 154. The second gadget that I would genuinely defend until the end of the earth is a microplane grater. I was bought one last year for my birthday, and was transported to another utopian dimension the first time I used it. I zest a lot of lemons, use an inordinate amount of nutmeg, and love to make clouds of Parmesan precipitate over pasta. This tool – this piece of genius culinary aid – offers the most efficient way to do all of this, and blows a normal box grater with a skruggy bit on one side for lemons and limes out of the water.

You don't need either of these two things to cook the vast majority of the recipes in this book, but if you did have a sudden urge to go and buy something, either of them is a smashingly tasteful purchase.

OVENS

Ovens are like cars. Each make and model handles differently, and you can never quite predict how well yours will behave until you try doing something dangerous like making a pavlova in it. Because of the discrepancies between age, models, temperaments, and whether Mercury is in retrograde or not, I only ever specify the temperature for a conventional oven; one where you'd bake a sponge cake at 180°C, do bread at 220°C, and whack everything else in somewhere in between. Please use my temperatures as a guide alongside the knowledge you have of your own oven: turn things down by 10–20 degrees if yours runs hot (or has a working fan-assist function), and up 10–20 degrees if you know it's a colder one. If you lack the aforementioned oven knowledge (and this is normal, by the way), then use my guidelines but keep an eye on things, checking regularly that you're not cremating your dinner or serving something that, after 40 minutes, has less colour than an untouched wheel of brie. If you're uncertain about all this and care lots, invest in an oven thermometer. If you're uncertain and don't care, then great. Me neither – all the markings have come off my dial and my oven thermometer exploded because I put it in cold water when it was still hot. You'll be grand.

ESSENTIAL SIDENOTES REGARDING FOOD CULTURE

OPINIONS

I have opinions about food. You have opinions about food. The world is big enough for these opinions to co-exist. I am loathe to upset people in real life, but this book may contain opinions you don't entirely agree with – so, like much of the food in here, do take everything I say with a pinch of salt. Additionally, I will always encourage you to play around with the recipes to suit your tastes, and will instruct you how to do so using substitutions and suggestions if you're not confident enough to give my initial advice the finger right off the bat. This, as much as I would like it to be, is not a Flisstatorship.

DIETS, HEALTH, NUTRIBOLLOCKS

Diets don't work, ingredients aren't magic, food is not medicine. Eat what makes you happiest.

The end.

A NOTE ON AUTHENTICITY

Cultural appropriation and authenticity are hotly debated topics in food and cookery, and for good reason: it'd be unfair for chefs to pilfer techniques and ingredients from someone else's culture and pass them off as their own for profit without acknowledgement. That'd be like painting a lovely picture, only for someone with better connections to come along, copy it and sell it to an upmarket gallery for some egregiously inflated price tag. And then piss in your paint pot on the way out.

In this book, I've been inspired by flavours and techniques from around the world and used them in a way that hopefully doth piss in no paint pot.

I've written recipes in a manner that makes sense for a UK-based twenty-something's budget, equipment and skillset, which sometimes means mixing and matching bits and bobs where needs be, and on occasion, clumping an entire subcontinent's worth of flavours together in accordance with what you can find in a budget supermarket. Therefore, I could *never* claim that my recipes that swing off these global ingredients and techniques are even remotely authentic. They're not a hundred-million miles off (I'm not making aubergine-free parmigiana here), but true authenticity, should such a concept exist, belongs to the nonnas and the omas and the aunties from whom these recipes originate. That's not to say that my versions aren't without merit; they're just not the whole story, and that needs to be acknowledged.

TAKE ME TO YOUR RECIPES, OH GLORIOUS SUPREME LEADER

That's the serious bits covered – it's joke after joke from here, plus you'll get a few recipes too. Cook from the heart, and if you don't have one of those, use your spleen. Have fun, pumpkins.

CHAPTER 1:
SPEEDY MCGREEDFACE

~~~~~~~~~~~~~~~~~~~~~~~~~~~~~~~~

Many full meals that look impressive on the pages of posh cookbooks come with the claim that you can cook them in under 30 minutes. When actually put to the test, these recipes induce the following response in your average joe: 'Bloody HELL. I've been in the kitchen for three days and this was only meant to take half an hour. The kids have eaten the table legs, and are about to start on the dog, and I've forgotten where I put the bloody salsa verde again.'

Hyperbole aside, such recipes exist because there is always a demand for a nice dinner, fast. With that in mind, the recipes in this chapter *actually* take 30 minutes or less, including prep time. They also don't use every bowl in the cupboard – and, more importantly, preserve a few brain cells in your weary little head to devote to more noble pursuits, such as staring at the cracks in the floorboards in hope that you can use The Force to magic out the £1 coin you just lost down there.

I can only apologise that this chapter consists of main dishes only, whereas other cookbooks may offer a starter, dessert and even a drink alongside a main. Mine don't come with any of that, because I can't fathom how you'd do all of it in under half an hour and not explode. My solution is to snaffle some crisps or olives while you're making dinner, have a glass of wine at the table, and then a Magnum for pudding. This counts as a worthy three-course feast if you squint a bit.

In terms of the following recipes, there should be something for everyone, and, as always, you can chop and change things as you see fit to suit your tastes and your budget. Some of the recipes are unusually formatted for your entertainment, so I hope you enjoy those. I will say now, before you write in, that the cheapest recipes in the book don't live here – you'll find them whispering to each other about the price of halloumi and fresh herbs in Chapter 4: Feed Your Friends (or Your Freezer).

The only other thing I wish to point out before you start is that if you can't find or don't have fresh parsley, don't substitute it with dried, because it ruins everything with its papery rubbishness. If you don't have parsley – or you hate it – use basil, and if you hate basil, then just use lemon zest and call it a day. If you hate lemon zest, parsley *and* basil, then I'm afraid you're a lost cause. Sorry.

PUFF PASTRY
PIZZA FLORENTINE Ⓥ

Do not tell the Italians that I'm calling this a pizza. They will come for me. Nonna will bash me with her rolling pin and Madre will pour hot espresso in my ears.

This simple tart[1] doesn't even have to be Florentine (whose two essential ingredients are eggs and spinach) if you don't want it to be, but it's a great starting point. The pastry also takes well to having mushrooms or peppers sliced and scattered over it, with a few finely sliced rings of red onion thrown on for bite. I've found that courgettes or aubergines make the pastry go soggy if you're adding them raw, but I'll wholly encourage their use here if they've been cooked first. Essentially, you can dress this up or down as you wish, and even use cream cheese or ricotta as a base rather than the tomato. If you really want to go wild, you can even do a Greek version with olives and feta, complete with an Oykos for pudding.

Serves 2 generously, takes 25 minutes

YOU'LL NEED:

½ small bag of spinach (around 50g)

a mug of soft veg, thinly sliced, such as ½ red pepper or 4–5 errant mushrooms and a few rings of onion if you have a half one lying around in the fridge

a roll of ready-made puff pastry (around 300g if you prefer to roll your own, love)

3–4 tablespoons of tomato passata[2] or posh tomato pasta sauce from a jar that your flatmate has left lying around (tinned chopped tomatoes are too clumsy and watery here, so don't use those)

dried mixed herbs (if you're using passata)

a ball of fresh mozzarella

4 eggs

salt and a black pepper grinder, preferably full of black peppercorns

OPTIONAL EXTRAS:

a few teaspoons of pesto, if it's open and needs using ASAP

OPTIONAL *FANCY* EXTRAS:

a sprinkle of shaved Parmesan

a couple of slices of Parma ham (very optional, very fancy)

a handful of rocket

Method this way ⟶

---

[1] Horribly relatable.

[2] Use the rest of the passata in place of a tin of tomatoes in the Massive Vegetarian Lasagne (page 112), Sweet Potato, Spinach and Chickpea Curry (page 107) or Accidental Cheap Ragu (page 126). Alternatively, make 15 of these tarts just for fun.

Preheat your oven to 210°C.

Find a microwavable bowl or dish that will fit all the spinach in it and zap it in the microwave on high for 1 minute or so while you chop any veg you're using. If you don't have a microwave, quickly pour boiling water over the spinach to wilt it, then drain it after 2 minutes. Leave the cooked spinach to cool for a moment while you finish your chopping, then squeeze out any water using your hands. Discard the water. Return the spinach to its bowl and let it sit and steam dry while you fiddle with the other stuff.

Unroll your pastry like a nice carpet onto a flat baking tray, using the pastry's own greaseproof paper as a means to save on washing-up. Then, as you would with any new rug, spread it with a thin but even layer of passata or tomato sauce, leaving a 1-inch border at the edges so you get nice crispy sides to dip in the egg yolk at the end. If you're using passata here, sprinkle it with a pinch of salt and some dried mixed herbs, but don't worry about doing that for the jarred sauce, which will be seasoned enough as it is.

Now drape your spinach over the base, spreading it about evenly. Scatter the other veg across the tart next, but make sure you're not using tonnes of it, as overloading the pastry will make it go soggy.

If you've got some pesto that needs using (don't worry if not), dot it around and about the veg, before tearing over the mozzarella. Grind over some black pepper, then bake for 18–20 minutes, or until the edges are just colouring.

When it's about 5–6 minutes off being ready, remove from the oven and, using a spoon, make 4 indentations where you'd like your eggs to sit. Crack them in, then return to the oven until the whites of the eggs are cooked but the yolks are still runny, and the edges of the tart are puffy and golden brown.

To serve, you can shave Parmesan all over the top, drape it with Parma ham, if using, or scatter it with rocket – or do two, three or none of those things until your wallet's content is content.

SMOKY TEX-MEX TOMATOES AND BEANS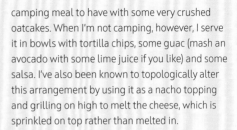

I first cobbled together this dish while wild camping in Scotland in November. It was around 2°C outside, and we needed something hot, filling and easy to source from the corner shop, which sold not much else besides tins and e-cigarettes. Not fancying a vape-liquid, spam and condom casserole, I came up with this, which utilised a packet of taco spices I had found at the bottom of my rucksack (obviously), coupled with a few bits and bobs from the long-life section of the convenience store. You'll probably have an easier time sourcing the ingredients, seeing as you're more likely to be in a house, in a town, near an actual shop, but it does make a great, filling camping meal to have with some very crushed oatcakes. When I'm not camping, however, I serve it in bowls with tortilla chips, some guac (mash an avocado with some lime juice if you like) and some salsa. I've also been known to topologically alter this arrangement by using it as a nacho topping and grilling on high to melt the cheese, which is sprinkled on top rather than melted in.

You can make it vegetarian by omitting the smoked bacon and instead using red onions fried slowly with smoked paprika.

Serves 2 generously, takes 10–15 minutes

YOU'LL NEED:

4 rashers of streaky smoked bacon, chopped into bits, or a packet of smoked lardons (alternatively, use a medium red onion and 2 teaspoons of smoked paprika mixed with a big pinch of salt)

vegetable or olive oil, for frying

a packet of fajita, taco or enchilada seasoning, GF if needed (or a teaspoon of smoked paprika, a teaspoon of dried oregano, a teaspoon of ground cumin, ½ teaspoon of chilli powder and ½ teaspoon of salt, mixed together)

a tin of chopped tomatoes

a tin of mixed beans in water, drained of their liquid (use cannellini beans if you can't get mixed)

a big handful of grated Cheddar cheese

OPTIONAL EXTRAS:

a handful of rocket, spinach, or kale

tortilla chips, GF if needed, to serve

guac, to serve

salsa, to serve

Start by frying off your bacon in a touch of oil in a medium-sized saucepan over a medium-high heat. Once the fat starts coming out of it, dump in the spice mix and fry it with the bacon for a minute or two. (If you're doing the veggie version, slice your onion into half-moons and fry in a generous amount of vegetable oil with the smoked paprika until slightly softened, around 7–8 minutes, then add the spice mix, then continue as below.)

Once everything is smelling fragrant, tip in the tin of tomatoes, followed by the beans. Stir to combine, then leave on high to boil through for 3–4 minutes. If it's looking too thick, add a splash of boiling water. Also, if you want to add something green and wiltable (rocket, spinach, kale) here, be my guest.

Taste and adjust for seasoning, then, just as you serve, stir through the handful of cheese, which should melt and turn pleasingly stringy as you use your tortilla chips to scoop the taco beans into your face, along with any guac or salsa you might fancy.

FRITTATA, BUT MAKE IT ABBA VO GFO

To be sung to the tune of 'Money, Money, Money' by ABBA. Actual recipe on next page.

I ROOT AROUND, THE CUPBOARD'S BARE, I THROW MY HANDS UP IN THE AIR
AIN'T THIS SAD!
THE LEAFLET FROM THE TAKEAWAY, IS BEGGING ME TO LOOK ITS WAY
NOT SO FAST!

'COS IN MY MIND I HAVE A PLAN
TO MAKE DINNER WITH JUST ONE PAN
I WOULDN'T EVEN HAVE TO BEG, 'COS IN MY FRIDGE I HAVE SOME EGG
DO-DE-DO-DE-DO-DE-DO-
DO-DE-DO-DE-DO-DE-DO-DOOOOOOO

RUNNY, RUNNY, RUNNY,
EGGS ARE FUNNY
IN A BOWL I'LL CRACK

RUNNY, RUNNY, RUNNY,
BEAT IT, SONNY
THEY'RE THE PERFECT SNACK

AHAAAAAAAAAAA-AAAAAAA-AAAAAAAAAAAAAAAAH
ALL THE THINGS I WILL ADD
WHILE MY EGGS ARE VERY RUNNY
IN THIS SKINT GIRL'S WORLD

I HEAT THE PAN UPON THE HOB, AND ADD SOME BUTTER, JUST A BLOB

AIN'T THAT FAST?

AND THEN I SOURCE SOME FROZEN PEAS, A SLICE OF HAM, SOME BROCCOLI

FROM WEEKS GONE PAST

I TIP THIS ALL INTO THE PAN

THEN POUR MY EGGS ROUND LIKE A SAVOURY FLAN

I'LL LET IT BUBBLE UP THE SIDES, THEN TURN THE HEAT DOWN WHILE TIME BIDES,

DO-DE-DO-DE-DO-DE-DO-

DO-DE-DO-DE-DO-DE-DO

RUNNY, RUNNY, RUNNY

EGGS AREN'T RUNNY

WHEN THEY'RE COOKED RIGHT THROUGH

MONEY, MONEY, MONEY

DON'T HAVE UNY

EGGS ARE CHEAP THOUGH, PHEW.

(ACTUAL) RECIPE VO GFO

Alright, alright, if you need a recipe for a frittata rather than just some hastily mashed-up song lyrics (see previous page), here's a basic guide. Everything except the eggs is optional, so sub in what you like. If you were wanting some inspo though, the frittata in the photo opposite has got feta, red peppers and leeks in it – a smashing combo if ever I saw one.

Serves as many as you wish (extremely customisable), takes about 10 minutes

YOU'LL NEED:

a selection of questionable leftovers (for example, odd bits of roast dinner or last night's kebab meat that you don't want to a) think about or b) throw away)

a teaspoon of butter or oil per egg

2–3 eggs per person, depending on how hungry you are

½ mug of frozen peas per person

salt

OPTIONAL EXTRAS:

possibly some cheese

chutney, to serve

bread

Find some leftovers that could be fried, and chop them up into small bits. I like to use cold cooked potatoes, bits of ham, the odd wrinkly pepper lurking at the bottom of the vegetable drawer and a few mashed-up pickled onions. You can, genuinely, use whatever – *whatever* – you like.

Heat a medium-sized non-stick frying pan over a medium heat and pop in the butter or oil. Crack the eggs into a bowl and season them while the fat heats up, stirring in any cheese, too, if you have it. When the pan's hot, add your leftovers and fry them until they've got a bit of colour on them and are heated through very well, so that any bacteria present will be smacked into oblivion. Add the frozen peas.

Now reduce the heat to medium-low and pour your eggs around your leftovers. If you've got a lid, now is the time to use it. If you don't, use a large dinner plate – or just leave the eggs uncovered in the full knowledge that you'll have to flip the frittata to cook it through.

Depending on the thickness of your frittata, the size of your pan and the quantity of leftovers, you might be able to get away with just leaving it for 5 minutes until the middle is cooked through, but if the edges are looking brown while the top and middle are raw, it's time to flippity-floppity. You can either do the very unromantic thing of cutting it in half in the pan (use wooden or plastic utensils on non-stick) and flipping each side separately, or you can try sliding it onto a chopping board or plate, then flopping it back in the other way up so it remains whole.

When the eggs are cooked through, slice the frittata and serve with chutney, or possibly in a sandwich if you have bread in the house. Now, go and watch *Mamma Mia*.

WARM BULGUR WHEAT, HALLOUMI AND HARISSA SALAD v

Bulgur wheat is one of those things that looks suspiciously expensive. But worry not, as if you go to the right place – specifically, your local Middle Eastern shop – you can pick up a kilo, dried, for around £1.25. This will make approximately 3 tonnes' worth when cooked, which, in my mind, is excellent value for money.

That said, although still fairly budget-friendly, this recipe actually comes out as one of the most expensive in the book, because it uses lots of fresh herbs and a whole block of halloumi. You *can* substitute the bulgur wheat for rice, and the halloumi for tofu, but it's the fresh herbs and harissa that really make it, so I'd not want to substitute those or it'd be something else entirely. You know what you can afford best.

I'll leave it up to you if you feel like adding something Ottolenghi-like, such as pomegranate seeds or a grated aged artisan chopping board, but a little bit of sweetness from some dried fruit does make this pop.

Serves 2 generously, takes 20 minutes

YOU WILL NEED:

¾ mug of coarse bulgur wheat (about 150g)

a block of halloumi

olive oil, for frying, plus an extra slug to serve

a tin of chickpeas, drained and tipped onto a pile of kitchen roll to soak up extra moisture

2 tablespoons of harissa paste

½ cucumber[1]

½ packet of coriander (25g);[2] use double the parsley if coriander tastes soapy to you, poor thing

½ packet of parsley (25g)[3]

a tablespoon of lemon juice (from a real-life lemon or a bottle   it doesn't matter)

salt

OPTIONAL EXTRAS:

2 tablespoons of either raisins, roughly chopped apricots or pomegranate seeds

Method this way ➡

[1] Use the rest in a big green salad to serve with literally anything.

[2] Use the rest to top Eve's Customisable Tomato and Butter Bean Stew (page 14).

[3] Every other recipe in this book uses fresh parsley, you won't be pushed to find a use for it.

WARM BULGUR WHEAT, HALLOUMI AND HARISSA SALAD CONTINUED ←

Start by cooking your bulgur wheat in a medium-sized pan over a high heat with around 2 mugs of boiling water and a big pinch of salt for about 10 minutes. Think of it like rice if you're unfamiliar.

While that's cooking, chop your halloumi into slices, then halve each one so you have a nice stack of squares. Fry off these squares in a large, shallow frying pan over a medium-high heat with a little splash of oil, working in batches if your pan is only wee. Drain any water that comes off the halloumi, as that'll massively slow down your browning, then increase the heat to high and fry the halloumi until golden, turning when you need to. Once both sides are golden, keep the pan on the heat but remove the cheese and set aside.

Add a little more oil to the now-empty pan if you need to, then tip in the chickpeas, followed by the harissa paste. Fry for 4–6 minutes, stirring to coat the chickpeas all over with the paste. Hopefully the chickpeas are dry enough not to spit, but watch out and stand back if that does happen. Leave this mixture over a medium heat, stirring occasionally, while you dice your cucumber and very finely chop your herbs.

By this time, your bulgur wheat should be cooked through – try it. It should have a little bite but still be soft. If there's any water left in the pan, drain it. Add the grains to a big serving bowl or mixing bowl. Next add the hot harissa chickpeas, stirring to coat everything nicely, then toss in your halloumi, your cucumbers, your chopped herbs and your fruit, if you're using it. Drizzle over a tiny slug of olive oil, followed by the lemon juice, and serve.

SEND NOODS (V) (DF)

This easy soup takes a packet of instant noodles and turns it into a full meal. It's for those days where you really, really want to just do nothing except stare at the nearest wall, but you know you should attempt to do yourself one nutrition. Please note that I'm absolutely no expert in East Asian cookery, so this is a very warped, anglicised version of some of the brothy noodle soups you might find there. It uses ingredients you could probably find in a corner shop in north Devon, so if you've got access to the proper stuff, such as dashi powder, edamame, nori or tea-stained eggs, then please do use them to your advantage.

Serves 1, takes 10 minutes

YOU'LL NEED:

veg oil, for frying

a garlic clove

2 spring onions

a value packet of instant ramen noodles

an egg, possibly two if you're hungry

2 tablespoons of soy sauce (I prefer dark, but use what you have)

a squirt of vinegary hot sauce – a tablespoon or so

a handful of salted peanuts, crushed or chopped a little

OPTIONAL EXTRAS:

a handful of any soft veg you like (mushrooms, peppers, beansprouts, etc.)

chilli flakes, if you have any

a little bit of freshly chopped chilli

sesame oil, if you have it

a lime wedge

Make sure you've got a freshly boiled kettle to start with to help speed things along.

Heat 1 teaspoon of the veg oil (not the sesame oil – that one is best for drizzling) in a small frying pan over a medium heat. Finely slice the garlic clove, then top and tail your spring onions and remove any outer layers you don't want to eat.

Now, separate the green hollow bits from the white bulbs – you'll be using both, just in separate bits of the dish. Finely slice the white bulbs into rounds and fry them in the oil, along with the garlic, until both are a little coloured, adding in any other veg you want cooked here. When the veg, garlic and onions are done, plonk them into the bowl you want to eat out of. Keep the frying pan hot and add a little extra veg oil, plus chilli flakes if you have any.

Now cook your noodles separately, along with their seasoning, in 400ml boiling water, rather than the amount specified on the packet. As soon as you've poured the water on the noodles, crack your eggs into the hot frying pan. I love crispy eggs, which is why I like to get my pan nice and hot. Then, after I've cracked them in, I pop a glass lid over the top (it doesn't matter if the lid doesn't fit the pan here, just as long as it goes over the egg). This makes sure that the top of the egg steams and cooks through and the bottom goes lacy and crisp, while still ensuring you get a runny yolk. If you don't want a crispy-bottomed egg, just fry it more slowly.

When your noodles are done, add the soy sauce and the hot sauce to the broth that they're cooking in, then slop everything into the serving bowl that already has your veg in it. Top with the egg(s), then slice and sprinkle over the green parts of the spring onions, along with the crushed peanuts. Finish with a drizzle of sesame oil, a little bit of fresh chilli and a squeeze of lime if you have it, and any other extras you feel would go well here, such as leftover roast chicken or some fried tofu.

PIMP MY MACKEREL ROCKET PESTO PASTA

This is another one of my camping recipes that also works incredibly well as a 10-minute meal at home. It's quick, easy, customisable, and tastes lovely and fresh due to the inordinate amount of lemon in it.

You can make this even cheaper by using frozen spinach instead of rocket – just add it before the peas so it cooks through in time. As well as using tinned fish, you can also omit the zest and use bottled lemon juice instead for a meal that is very easy on the bank account – and actually good for you while we're at it.

Sprinting in the other direction, though, if you wanted to make it a bit richer, a dollop of mascarpone or cream cheese works very nicely melted into the pasta straight after draining. Using hot-smoked mackerel takes it up a notch, too.

Serves 2, takes 10–15 minutes

YOU'LL NEED:

enough pasta for 2 (200g) – fusilli works best, followed by penne or rigatoni; don't use long pasta here if you can help it

2 tins of mackerel in sunflower oil, or 2–3 smoked mackerel fillets from a vacuum packet if you're feeling bougie

a small lemon

½ mug of frozen peas (or a few bite-sized broccoli florets if you're camping)

a small bag of rocket (about 50g)

a small jar of green pesto sauce (about 200g)

salt and oodles of freshly ground black pepper

OPTIONAL EXTRAS:

a dollop of cream cheese or mascarpone

Start by cooking your pasta according to the packet instructions in plenty of boiling, salty water.

Meanwhile, in a bowl, break up the mackerel using a fork (drain it first if it's in oil, and remove the skins if you're using the smoked stuff). Mix in the black pepper, then zest the lemon over the top before mashing that in, too. (If you're camping, you *can* just plop everything together in the same pan at the end, but you might squish your pasta a bit trying to break up the fish fillets, so use a separate bowl if you can.)

Just as the pasta is reaching al dente, tip in your peas. Now for the clever bit. Pop half the rocket into the colander or sieve[1] that you're going to drain your pasta through, then drain the pasta as normal. The rocket will wilt as the water rushes over it.

When you've drained the pasta, return it to the pan. You'll now need to work quickly so that your pasta doesn't lose too much heat. Add the pesto, the lemony mackerel and the rest of the rocket (plus any cream cheese if you're using it). Stir it all around until everything is evenly distributed, then squeeze over the juice of the whole lemon to cut through the oiliness of the pesto and the mackerel and give it some real zing.

If I make this when I'm camping, I just hand my tent-mate a fork at this point, and we both eat out of the same pan. You can be a non-savage and put it in bowls, if you like.

---

[1] If you don't have either of those things and tend to drain your pasta against the side of the sink, or using the saucepan lid, just put the rocket in the water *immediately* before you drain the pasta so it wilts properly. The reason we wilt some of the rocket and leave some fresh to add at the end is to give a contrasting texture, and because it looks good.

ONE-PAN SALADE NIÇOISE DF GF

For those of you not in the know, salade niçoise is basically a random cupboard dinner pimped out with bits of lettuce. It's a mixture of tinned tuna, black olives, a few strips of anchovies, some jammy boiled eggs and some boiled potatoes, tossed with green stuff. The French have a knack for putting delicious things together (for example, wine and cheese, cheese and wine, cheese and cheese, wine and wine), and this hearty salad, which originates from Nice, just so happens to be another example of such synergy.

This is my speedy version, in which you cook the eggs, the potatoes and the green beans in the same pan of water, just for different amounts of time. It's a light yet satisfying weeknight meal. You can leave out the anchovies or olives if you have little baby tastebuds that need some more time to appreciate the finer things in life.

Serves 2 generously, takes 20 minutes

YOU'LL NEED:

4 smallish floury potatoes or 6–8 waxy ones, depending on what you prefer or what's in season

a mug of fresh or frozen green beans

a romaine lettuce

a mug of cherry tomatoes

6 anchovy fillets from a tin[1]

as many pitted black olives as you want, or none if you don't

a tin of tuna, drained

a tablespoon of lemon juice, either from real-boy lemon or from a bottle, plus extra to serve

6 eggs

nice olive oil that hasn't lost its virginity, for drizzling

salt and freshly ground black pepper

Chop your potatoes into smallish chunks (or quarters if they're wee ones) and throw them into a pan of salty boiling water. (Oh, just a note: if I ever peel a tattie, I'll get a tattoo to commemorate the event.)

While the potatoes are having fun in the saline jacuzzi, top and tail your green beans (if they're fresh) before halving them. Chop up the romaine lettuce and put it in a big serving bowl. Halve your cherry tomatoes and add them to the bowl, too. Tear over the anchovy fillets and plonk in the olives. Dump in the tin of tuna. Sprinkle the lemon juice over everything. Think of some more creative imperatives.

When your tatties have been boiling for around 10 minutes, plop your whole eggs into the water alongside them, along with the green beans (I've always found green beans take an absolute age to cook through in comparison to other green veg, so it works adding everything at this stage). Continue to boil all of this for a further 7 minutes – this is one of the few times I'll ask you to set a timer on your phone, as it's easy to over-do the eggs.

[1] Use the rest of the anchovies in the Impressive Shallot Tarte Tatin (page 63) or cook with fried onions as a base for the Beef and Stout Stew-Pie (page 123).

When the potatoes are properly soft, drain everything into a big colander and remove the eggs. Plunge them into a cereal bowl of cold water so that you don't destroy your fingers trying to peel them while hot. They should be cooked through but still a bit jammy in the middle when you cut them into halves, which is what you should do next. Set aside to put on top of the salad, or the yolks will fall out everywhere when you toss it.

The potatoes and green beans will have cooled down a little in the time it's taken you to peel the eggs, so you can add them to the bowl with the lettuce now. Drizzle everything generously with olive oil, sprinkle with some salt and black pepper and toss everything with the wrong end of the salad tossers for maximum authenticity. Spoon out onto plates and top with the egg halves.

Serve with side-eye and an extra spritz of lemon.

LIMERICK SEAFOOD LINGUINE

Have the recipe description in a series of limericks – you're SO welcome. Actual recipe on the next page.

IMAGINE YOU NEEDED TO BRING
TO YOUR TABLE, A TASTE OF THE SPRING
WHAT WOULD YOU FAVOUR, TO GIVE YOU THAT FLAVOUR?
A LEMONY PASTA DISH THING?

MY BOYFRIEND SAID LOUDLY: 'HEAR, HEAR;
NOW, THAT IS A CRACKING IDEA.'
I LISTED THE ITEMS I'D BUY TO DELIGHT 'EM,
AND HE NODDED, SAYING, 'DON'T FORGET BEER.'

I RETURNED FROM THE HUSTLE AND BUSTLE
WITH PARSLEY AND LEMON AND MUSSELS,
THIS WOULDN'T TAKE LONG, IF IT DIDN'T GO WRONG,
AND WITH ANY LUCK, WON'T BE A FUSSLE.

AFTER WE PUT ON THE PASTA,
(THE SAUCE WOULDN'T TAKE LONG TO MASTER)
I HEATED SOME BUTTER – OH, LOTS – DID I STUTTER?
AND FRIED GARLIC AND CHERRY TOMATA.

WHEN EVERYTHING'S JUST TURNING BROWN,
IT'S TIME TO TAKE LEMON TO TOWN
THE JUICE AND THE ZEST MAKE THE FLAVOUR THE BEST
NOW ADD SALT AND YOU'LL HAVE THIS THING DOWN.

I IMPLORE ALL MY READERS: DON'T JUDGE,
I AM POOR AND YOU MUSTN'T BEGRUDGE
THAT MY MUSSELS CAME PRE-CLEANED, AND PRE-WASHED, AND PRE-STEAMED:
THEY ARRIVED IN A WINE AND CREAM SLUDGE.

I EMPTIED THIS PACKET, I DID
INTO MY PAN, AND I PUT ON A LID
WITH A LITTLE GOOD SHUGGLING, AND SOME CHILLI - A SMUDGELING -
ALL WILL BE JUST PERFECT, KIDS.

WHEN THE PASTA WAS TOUCHING AL DENTE
AND THE LIGHT SAUCE WAS BUBBLING PLENTY
I STIRRED IN THE LINGUINE TO MAKE IT ALL CREAMY
AND CHOPPED PARSLEY SO FINE IT WENT SCENTY.

ONCE ALL THE PARSLEY WAS SCATTERED
ONLY THE SERVING NOW MATTERED
I SPOONED ONTO PLATES (NOT BOWLS; PLEASE NO HATE)
AND SQUEEZED OVER MORE LEMON - A SMATTER.

WHEN THE BOYFRIEND AND I DID TUCK IN,
OUR FACES TRANSFORMED INTO GRINS
'THIS MUSSEL LINGUINE IS THE BEST THAT I'VE SEENIE,'
BEAMED MY PARTNER, WITH SAUCE DOWN HIS CHIN

FOR THOSE KEEN CHEFS WHO JUST WANT TO KNOW
THE RECIPE'S IN FULL BELOW
IT'S REALLY QUITE HARD; TO COOK, AND TO BARD
SO I'LL SEE MYSELF OUT - YES - I'LL GO.

(ACTUAL) RECIPE DFO

Just in case you couldn't follow it as a series of limericks (see previous page), here's the recipe formatted as, yanno, an actual recipe. As an aside, this might actually be my favourite dish in the book – it's creamy, zesty and herby all at once, and it's super quick to make too. But don't tell Eton Mess (page 145) I said that. She'll only get jealous.

Serves 2, takes 15 minutes

YOU'LL NEED:

enough linguine for 2 (2 portions will fit in the 'o' shape you can make with your thumb and index finger)

a mug full of cherry tomatoes

2–3 garlic cloves if they're small, just 1 if it's really fat

a pinch of chilli flakes, or ½ mild red chilli

an actual whole bunch/packet of fresh parsley (30g or so)

3 generous tablespoons of either butter or olive oil

zest and juice of a large lemon (roughly 2 teaspoons of zest and 30ml/2 tablespoons of juice)

a packet (450g) of refrigerated vacuum-packed mussels in white wine sauce (they're dead cheap at Lidl and Aldi)

salt

Start by cooking your pasta according to the packet instructions in lots of salted water in the largest pan you have. Salting the water seasons the pasta from the inside out and makes it better in every conceivable manner. I will send you ants in the post if I find out you don't salt your pasta water.

Chop your cherry tomatoes in half, chop your garlic into very small pieces (don't crush it, though, or make it into a paste) and finely chop the chilli (if you're using fresh). Separate the leaves from the stems of the parsley. Keeping them separate, finely chop both.

Melt the butter or heat the oil in the largest frying pan you have over a medium heat. Add the cherry tomatoes, garlic, chilli flakes or chopped chilli, chopped parsley stalks and a little pinch of salt. Fry everything very gently for a few minutes, until just colouring. When it's got a little bit of brown on it, add the lemon zest. Add half the lemon juice and let everything get to know each other a wee bit.

Now, tear open the mussels packet and empty them straight into the pan. Mix everything together – the mussel juices should go a pale pinkish colour from mixing with the tomatoes. Add most of the rest of the lemon juice, reserving a tiny bit for the end. Shuggle it about a bit and pop the lid on, then leave for 5 minutes until the mussels heat through.

Your pasta should be near enough done by now. To make it absolutely perfect, you want to take it out just as it's on the verge of al dente, because when you stir it through the mussels, it'll finish cooking and soak up some of the lovely zesty sauce. I don't bother draining it; I just spoon it with a pair of tongs straight into the mussel pan. This has the added advantage of taking some of the starchy pasta water with it, which thickens the sauce slightly. If you've decided to drain using a colander, remember to add a tablespoon or so of pasta water to the sauce before you drain it down the sink.

Make sure your parsley leaves are chopped very finely, then stir them through the pasta. To serve, scatter over a wee extra bit of the parsley, which will have inevitably clung to the chopping board, give it all a final squeeze of lemon, and plonk in the middle of the table with some deep plate-bowls and a dish for the empty shells.

5 THINGS TO DO WITH POTATOES

Boil 'em, mash 'em, stick 'em in your shoes: tatties, or potatoes if you're proper, should win an award for services to happiness. They're also as cheap as raw chips, so why not make use of them by trying out one of the below loosely constructed recipe ideas? Two quick notes before we start, though:

Don't attempt to make mash with small waxy potatoes. It won't work, and you'll be left with a sad pile of gloop. Use big floury ones for mash, chips, jackets and cricket. Use small waxy ones for salads, to have plain with obscene quantities of butter, and for clogging up marble runs.

I have not willingly peeled a tatty since 2012. You may choose to remove the skin, of course – do what you like – but just giving them a quick rinse or a scrub to get anything weird off works just fine. And really don't bother peeling baby ones; that's just a waste of time for everyone, including the potato.

1. SPICY DICEY SPUDLINGS VG GF

Take 2 fist-sized **floury potatoes** per person and cut them up into large dice (around an inch cubed, or 25,400 cubic microns if you're more comfortable with metric units). Preheat the oven to 220°C and glug a big bit of **veg oil** into a flat baking tray that is big enough to house all the potatoes in one layer – this is important for crispy browning. Heat up the oily tray in the oven while you par-boil your spuds for in a vat of salted water for 10 minutes.

Drain the spuds thoroughly, then return them to the saucepan and give them a shake with a drizzle of oil, a tablespoon of **curry powder**, a teaspoon of **cumin**, **salt** and lashings of **black pepper**. Remove the tray from the oven and sprinkle another teaspoon of curry powder over the oil, then tip your tatties in, giving it all a good old toss as you go. Bake for 20-30 minutes, or until everything is looking golden, shuggling a bit now and again. Serve with Spatchcocked Chicken (page 43) and Quick Pickled Onions (page 77).

2. CREAMY DREAMY MISHMASH

This is my fairly basic recipe for mashed potatoes, because it's useful to know if you've not attempted it before. Allow 3 medium **floury potatoes** per person (you may have leftovers), and chop them up into rough chunks, skin off or on, depending on what you prefer. Pop them in a giant saucepan on the stove and cover them with boiling water and a generous sprinkle of **salt.** Let them boil until they're *completely* soft in the centre, then drain thoroughly before mashing with roughly 1 tablespoon of **salted butter** per person, plus 2 tablespoons of **milk** per person. You can stir through a touch of **wholegrain mustard** or some **horseradish** if you like. Taste it and ask yourself if it needs more salt – it should be OK, given the butter and salted boiling water, but do have a check anyway.

If you don't have a potato masher, give the pan to your hench friend with a fork and tell them to have at it – this works, and I have used this method on more than one occasion. Any leftovers can be mixed with a couple of eggs and fried into delicious patties, by the way.

3. HASSLE YE BACK
GF VGO

By hassling the backs of your potatoes, you're making the surface area available to butter or olive oil much larger, which is only a good thing. Make slits around the width of a pound coin all the way along the tops of the **tatties**. Make sure the slits run deep, but not all the way through, so the potato looks like it has vertebrae and a spine, if you get me. Once slat, cover everything with **salt** and **oil** and bake the tatties for around 40–45 minutes at 190°C. When they're soft all the way through and the hasselback bits are crispy, mix a couple of tablespoons of **melted butter** with some **chilli flakes** and fresh **parsley**, and brush or drizzle that over the tatties before serving. You could even roast a head of garlic along with the tatties – just pop it in for the last 20 minutes of baking – then mix a few of the golden cloves in with the butter. But maybe that could be complicating things – I'll leave it up to you.

4. SQUISH POPS

Both waxy potatoes or very small floury potatoes work fine here, but make sure they're no bigger than a lime, or they won't do as well. This does take a little more time than just boiling or mashing, but they're so lovely that it's worth it.

Throw roughly 5–6 **potatoes** per person into a large pot of salted water and boil the ever-loving crap out of them for a good 20 minutes, or until they're really quite soft. Preheat the oven to 200°C, then thoroughly drain the tatties, spreading them out on a baking sheet and leaving for 10 minutes to steam and get as dry as possible (this is so they get crispier).

Next, take a mug and squish them with the bottom of it, so they look like little splats. Drizzle them very generously with **olive or vegetable oil** then sprinkle over some **flaky sea salt** if you have it (use normal if not) before whacking the potatoes into the hot oven for at least 25 minutes or until golden. I like to dip them in **tomato and chilli chutney** because I'm posh, but **ketchup** goes equally well.

5. TENDRIL COMPETITION

Give each player one **potato** each. Whoever's potato grows the longest tendril at the end of one month is the winner. Plant the potatoes in a public park flowerbed afterwards for maximum enjoyment.

CHAPTER 2:
NICE NORMAL DINNERS FOR TWO HUNGRY PEOPLE

~~~~~~~~~~~~~~~~~~~~

I often wonder what it might be like to be a python. Pythons don't have to cook dinner, day in, day out. They can simply strangle a gazelle, yomp the whole thing in one and not have to eat again for a week or two. What's most impressive, though, is that they don't get bored of it, either. You'll never find a baby python complaining at the dinner tree: 'But we had gazelle last week. I want antelope!' in the same manner that my brother and I would sigh and roll our eyes when it was shepherd's pie for every other meal. Gosh, what we would have given for a bit of gazelle.

Where I'm going with this rather scenic introduction is that we *Homo sapiens* are sort of required to eat dinner every day. And it's nice for us to have a bit of variety in what we shovel down. All too often, however, we fall into a rut of eating the same things over and over again, so I'm hoping that this chapter will provide a little trickle of din-spiration (yes, that's a portmanteau; you're welcome) into your daily routine. As always, if there's an unfamiliar ingredient, then I'll let you know how to deal with it, and suggest ways to use it up in the footnotes.

Lots of these recipes take around 15–20 minutes of hands-on time, followed by the odd bit of stirring, or a romantic mini-break in a hot oven. The majority take around an hour in total, but some take much less. And, of course, some dishes are a tad more involved than others, but I'll point that out where it's needed – just read the recipe through first to find out how much effort will be required of you. All said and done, though, the meals here really aren't too difficult if you have a couple of brain cells to rub together.

My top tip for cooking dinner without it seeming like a chore is to make yourself a nice drink (I like either posh herbal infusions or a very cold white wine, depending on the day) and put on some tunes. This is you-time, unless you want to share it – and if you do, phone a friend and natter away, blasting them on speaker mode while you fry onions. Or corner a flatmate and coerce them into telling you about their day.

These recipes feed two happily, but if it's just you, then make it all anyway and have the other half for lunch tomorrow – they all work this way except the pancakes (page 51), where you should just halve the batter if you're cooking for one. So, to dinner we go, and what fun we shall have. And sorry there's no antelope.

SPATCHCOCKED CHICKEN IN THE DEAD OF NIGHT (GF)

Sing it like The Beatles' song, go on.

This is my favourite way of cooking a whole chicken. For those of you who don't know, spatchcocking is when you open up a chicken like some sort of morbid book. By removing the backbone and spreading out the bird on a baking tray, you increase the surface area of the chicken, enabling it to cook much more quickly, while getting crispy skin all over. This particular spatchcock recipe uses Indian-inspired spice paste, so it's obviously great with the Spicy Dicey Spudlings (page 38), which you can dip gluttonously into the fragrant chicken fat. You can, of course, use whatever seasoning you like instead of the spice paste, rubbing it into the chicken before you cook it – Cajun-style seasoning works well, and sometimes I'll do a simple lemon zest, chilli, salt and black pepper number instead. And don't throw away the backbone, either – roast it alongside the chicken, then let it cool and put it in your bone-bag in the freezer to make stock (see page 71).

The last thing I'll say about this recipe is that if you can leave the chicken to sit with the paste all over it for half an hour (or longer) before cooking it, you'll get properly seasoned, tender meat that is fully flavoured throughout.

Serves 2 as a centrepiece, takes 10 minutes hands-on work and 35 minutes to cook, plus 30 minutes optional marinating time

YOU'LL NEED:

a whole slippery chicken

a heaped teaspoon of salt

½ jar of tikka paste, or one of those small Patak's spice pots

To start, flip the poor chicken onto its back, so the breasts are counter-side down. Then, take a pair of large, clean kitchen scissors and remove the backbone, which should be facing up if you've chosen an anatomically correct chicken. I do this one side at a time, making two long, large cuts along each side of the spine. Cut it off at the end, near where the wishbone is.

Next, you want to flip the chicken back to being breast-side up. You'll notice it'll have lost some of its structural integrity, but so would you if someone cut your backbone out.

Now it's time to open out the chicken as you would the doors on a wardrobe, with the legs splayed out in front of everything. If you're being met with some resistance, take the heel of your hand and push down on the thickest part of the breast to break the breast-plate. This is pure, unadulterated masochism, and may not be suitable for those with a weak disposition or a tendency towards cold-blooded murder. Crunch, crunch, motherclucker.[1]

Once your chicken is splayed to a relatively even thickness, make three long, slashes in each breast, about 1cm deep, plus two in each thigh. Next, cover the whole thing with the salt, followed by the curry paste, which you should rub all over the chicken with your hands, getting under the skin of the thighs and breasts, and not forgetting about the inner cavity either. Doing this should feel like rubbing gunge into distinctly cold, wet armpits, but don't worry; your gruesome efforts will be rewarded in due course.

---

[1] If you're more of a visual learner, you can hop on to YouTube for a more detailed spatchcocking tutorial.

SPATCHCOCKED CHICKEN IN THE DEAD OF NIGHT CONTINUED ⟵

If you have time, let the chicken sit for 30 minutes (or longer) so everything can permeate. When you're ready, preheat the oven to 190°C and bake the chicken in a roasting tin, breast-side up, for about 35–40 minutes. We have a habit of overcooking chicken in the UK, so do check it after 35 minutes. You'll know it's cooked when a knife inserted into the thigh returns clear juices, rather than anything tinged with pink or red.

Let the chicken rest for 5 minutes out of the oven so that the meat fibres relax, then serve with something potatoey (see page 38 for the Spicey Dicey Spudlings in the photo) and some nice greens.

EASY STUFFED SEASONAL SQUASHES WITH MUSHROOMS, GRAINS AND HERBS VG GFO

If you're feeding vegans, or happen to swing that way yourself, this is a beautiful meal that makes great use of those cute little squashes that come into season in the winter. It feeds two very happily, but you can also use it as a centrepiece for a meatless roast dinner, splitting this recipe between four if you've got enough sides. To speed up the whole shebang, pop the hollowed-out squashes in the microwave for 15 minutes while you make the filling. If you don't have a microwave, firstly, go find one on Facebook Marketplace, because they're so useful. But if that part of the electromagnetic spectrum is simply too much for you to consider, then bake the squash in the oven without the filling for an extra 20 minutes.

Serves 2, takes a little over an hour

YOU'LL NEED:

2 little, cute, tiny baby squashes or pumpkins, roughly the size of an enormous grapefruit or a small bantam hen, whichever you're more familiar with

a very large white onion, or 2 medium ones

olive oil

a teaspoon each of dried rosemary and thyme, plus ½ teaspoon of dried sage

a 400g pack of mushrooms

a packet of those precooked-grain type things, GF if needed (250g);[1] if they're too expensive, then a tin of green lentils, drained, will do

a glug of white wine (about 75ml), or 60ml water and a tablespoon of vinegar

salt and freshly ground pepper

OPTIONAL EXTRAS:

fresh thyme leaves

Start by preparing the squash. It's just like doing a Halloween pumpkin, but on a smaller scale and without the face. Make a lid with a knife, then remove its guts and scrape out the centre and sides.[2] Pierce the squash skins a little with a knife, then pop them both in the microwave for 15 minutes, without their lids. If they don't fit in side by side, do them one at a time, for 8 minutes each.

Preheat the oven to 180°C.

While your squash are revolving, finely chop your onion(s) and fry in a good couple of tablespoons of olive oil, along with a pinch of salt, a good grinding of black pepper and the dried herbs, over a medium heat. While that's schmoozing, chop your mushrooms into roughly 1cm cubes.

---

[1] I like the quinoa ones because they make me feel very healthyful and have some protein in them, but the lentil ones are good too.

[2] Keep the seeds and toast them with salt and smoked paprika if you want a snack, but this is a little extra faff.

EASY STUFFED SEASONAL SQUASHES WITH MUSHROOMS, GRAINS AND HERBS CONTINUED ←—————

When the onions are soft, add another big glug of olive oil and tip in your mushrooms, which will soak up the oil like sponges, then shrink down as the water cooks out of them. Keep cooking until the mushrooms have got some nice bits of colour on them; this should take around 15 minutes. If you're using the fresh thyme, add the leaves now.

When your mushrooms are looking gucci, tip in your grains or lentils, then add the wine or vinegar water and a splash of boiling water if it's all looking a bit dry. Cook for 5–8 minutes to heat everything through, then taste for seasoning. Next, pull your squashes out of the microwave (careful, they're hot) and place on a baking tray, then spoon in the filling.[3] Pop the lids on precariously, then bake for half an hour, or until the flesh of the squash is tender to the point of a knife.

Serve as is, or with some extra green veg for fun.

---

[3] If you have too much filling for your squash, don't stress. Simply eat the filling by itself for lunch, or top it with some vegan puff pastry and make mini pies, or put it in a toastie with vegan cheese, or have it spooned over a jacket tattie. The world is your (vegan) oyster.

EVE'S CUSTOMISABLE TOMATO AND BUTTER BEAN STEW VG GF

Let me tell you a story about my good friend Eve.

When Eve arrived at university, she couldn't work out how to melt cheese onto her toast. The microwave made the bread soggy, the toaster was 90 degrees too upright, and the oven took bloody ages. Eventually, a friend called Lucy showed Eve how the grill worked. Eve was grill-thrilled, and from then on made countless rounds of cheese on toast, often accompanied by baked beans and a few handfuls of spinach, for *every single meal*.

By second year, Eve had grown bored of spinach-eggs-cheese-and-beans on toast. She needed something more exciting, so Lucy and I, her new flatmates, introduced her to onions and garlic, told her how cheap tinned tomatoes were, and explained roughly which herbs and spices worked well together. Fast forward four years, and Eve would say that getting a first-class degree in mathematics and then going straight into a well-paid civil servant role is her greatest achievement. I think it's making the leap from not being able to make cheese on toast to cooking fish pies, nut roasts, curries and stews from scratch, without a recipe. And this is the dish that started it all.

Serves 2, takes 30 minutes

YOU'LL NEED:

a large red onion, or 2 smaller ones

a good glug of olive oil

a teaspoon each of paprika, dried basil, dried oregano or any random selection of herbs your flatmates have acquired and you are hoovering up

2 garlic cloves

a big carrot and/or half a head of broccoli or 2 mugs of any other veg you like, such as red pepper or courgette

a couple of splashes of boiling water

a tin of chopped tomatoes

a squeeze of tomato purée (around a tablespoon)

a tin of butter beans, drained

½ small bag of spinach

salt and freshly ground black pepper

Roughly chop your onions into 1cm dice or slice them into thin rings. Fry them in a frying pan over a medium heat with the olive oil, along with a pinch of salt, some black pepper and your herbs and spices. Give the onions a few minutes to soften, then chop the garlic into tiny bits and pop that into the pan, too. Roughly chop your carrots into 1cm dice and add them to the pan, along with a splash of boiling water, then pop on a lid if you have one, turn the heat down to lowish, and make sure everything goes soft for about 10–15 minutes. If you're in a hurry, pop the carrots in the microwave for 5 minutes before adding, then just stir through.

Next, add your tin of chopped tomatoes and the tomato purée, along with another splash of water from the kettle, plus the broccoli or any chopped-up soft veg you might have. Stir in the butter beans and cover once more, then leave to simmer for 10 minutes. Right at the end, stir through the spinach until it wilts. Taste for seasoning, then serve.

. . . .

I like this stew a bit soupier, so I make it thinner with a bit of stock and add little mini elbow pasta shapes, but Eve likes it in its original thicc format, served with bread. If she's been to the gym, she'll have it with two hard-boiled eggs perched on top for extra gainz, which I find simply hilarious.

. . . .

EGGS IN TOMATO AND RED PEPPER SAUCE (VO) (GF) (DF)

In my second year of university, I thought I was a genius for putting eggs into a thick red pepper and tomato sauce to cook slowly on the stove. Turns out that folk in the Middle East have been doing this for aeons, and it's called shakshuka. Fliss: 0, History: 1. This is my own take, because there are countless versions out there. The chorizo is optional, but I love the smokiness that it brings.

If you're making the full amount, do it in the biggest frying pan you've got, and improvise with a baking sheet for a lid should you not have one that fits already. For bonus lazy points, eat it out of the pan and save on washing-up.

This recipe serves two hungry people very generously; add bread and greens, and it serves three to four less-hungry people moderately.

Serves 2–4 (see above), takes 25 minutes

YOU'LL NEED:

a medium red onion

½ chorizo ring (optional)

olive oil

2 fat garlic cloves, or 3 normal ones

2 peppers; red works best, but use what you've got

a pinch of chilli flakes (up to a teaspoon – those guys run hot)

a teaspoon of smoked paprika

2 tins of chopped tomatoes

4 eggs

salt

bread and butter, to serve (optional)

Start by slicing your onion and chopping your chorizo (if you're using it). Add them to a frying pan over a medium-high heat with a glug of oil.

When the onion is translucent and the chorizo is leaking its red oil pleasingly all over the place, finely chop the garlic and stir it in.[1] Once the garlic looks golden, thinly slice your red peppers and add them, too. Add the chilli flakes, paprika and salt and let everything schmooze for a hot minute.

Next, pour in your tomatoes and have everything come to a simmer. Taste it – it might need some more salt, but this depends on your preference, and whether or not you're using the chorizo.

Using the back of a big spoon, make little pockets in the sauce for the eggs to sit in, then crack them in carefully. Season the eggs too, or they'll be boring. Cover with a lid and then either let it sit for 10–15 minutes on the stove, or, if you haven't got that sort if time, thwack it under a hot grill for 5 – and don't melt the pan handle while you're doing it.

When the egg whites are cooked through but the yolks are still runny, plonk the pan in the middle of the table as a sharing dish with a load of bakely freshed bread and butter.

[1] Note that I'll never ask you to fry onions and garlic at exactly the same time. Garlic has a much higher sugar content, which makes it very easy to burn before the onions have even had a chance to go soft.

LEEK, GRUYÈRE AND BACON PANCAKES

I have a habit of becoming very bored of things very quickly, but pancakes will never be one of them. This is truly an outrageous recipe to have on a weeknight, but it's all the more fun because of it. The novelty of having savoury pancakes has not yet been lost for me, and the cheesy, bacon-y, leek-y filling really goes down well after a long, hard day of being on the internet.

The filling is deliciously easy, and sort of cooks itself once you've got the bacon bits rolling along. The time-taker here is the pancakes, but they're mostly foolproof if you've got a bit of common sense about you, and a desire to do something repetitive and all-consuming for 25 minutes. The pancake mix makes about 8–10 pancakes, so cook them all off, keep them warm, then have the last couple for pudding. I like to microwave a little ramekin of blackcurrant jam for 30 seconds, add a squish of lemon juice and pretend I've made compote before slathering that all over pancakes with a dob or two of extra-thick 10 per cent fat Greek yogurt.

Serves 2, takes 45 minutes

YOU'LL NEED:

For the pancakes

110g flour[1] (around a mug's worth)

2 eggs

250ml milk mixed with 50ml water[2] (¾ mug of milk, topped up with water)

a tablespoon of vegetable oil, plus more for cooking the pancakes

salt

For the cheesy pea-and-bacon filling

a pack of pancetta or bacon lardons; failing that, 5 bacon rashers, chopped into cubes

a big leek

a blodge of butter

a palm-sized wodge of Gruyère, or you can use strong Cheddar if you prefer

a mug of frozen peas

heaps of freshly ground black pepper

OPTIONAL EXTRAS:

your favourite dried herbs

Make the pancake batter first. Add the flour to a large-ish bowl, make a wee dip in the flour and crack the eggs into it. Stir the eggs into the flour with a fork or a balloon whisk until you have a thick batter. If it's too thick to stir, add a splash of the milk mixture. Add the milk and water little by little – you might need more or less than specified, but what you're aiming for is a thinnish batter; thinner than double cream, but not by much. Blend the tablespoon of oil into the batter, mixing well for full emulsification. Add a pinch of salt and any herbs you like. Bear in mind that if you're doing a pudding one, you can reserve half a mug of batter before adding the herbs, just to keep things separate.

[1] Plain flour is perfect, a 50/50 mix of plain and wholemeal works nicely, and self-raising flour works fine, too – you'll get slightly bubblier pancakes, but it's really not that noticeable.

[2] The water makes the pancakes lacier.

LEEK, GRUYÈRE AND BACON PANCAKES CONTINUED ⟵

Preheat the oven to the lowest possible setting, just to keep the pancakes warm as they hop off the stove.

Now take out a large frying pan and place over a low heat. Tip in the bacon lardons – you don't have to wait for the pan to heat up for this, because you want to fry the lardons slowly at first so all the fat comes out. Chop the leek into thin rings, and add to the pan once there's enough fat from the bacon lardons. Increase the heat to medium and add a blodge of butter.

Now heat a non-stick, ovenproof frying pan over a high heat and begin frying your pancakes while keeping an eye on the leeks and bacon. This takes some multitasking, as the pancakes do cook quickly. By the way, if you've not cooked pancakes before, here's how you do it: add a couple of tablespoons of batter to a hot, lightly oiled frying pan and swirl it around to coat the bottom evenly. Leave it for a minute or two, or until the edges are turning golden when you peek underneath, then flip carefully using a fish-slice to cook the other side. Don't worry if the first pancake is terrible; much like siblings, the first one tends to be a practice run.

Meanwhile, grate the Gruyère on the finer side of a grater. Shuggle the pan containing the leeks and lardons, making sure that everything is getting to know each other, and perhaps adding some black pepper if you like. Keep both pans going, sliding all the cooked pancakes onto a plate in the oven to stay warm, and making sure the leeks and bacon are colouring nicely.

When the bacon is nice and brown, and the leeks are just cooked, add your peas. They'll defrost very quickly and go a lurid shade of green. When they're completely warmed through, shuggle the pan again so that everything is in an even layer. Now, sprinkle the finely grated Gruyère over the leek mixture and keep it on the heat until it's *just* melted. Transfer the pan to the base of the lightly warmed oven while you cook the rest of the pancakes – there should only be about a few to go now. The cheese should go delightfully oozy in the meantime.

To serve, dump the filling pan and the plate of pancakes on the table. Scoop lines of the bacon and leek mixture into the centre of each pancake and swaddle with the edges. If you're being polite, use a knife and fork to eat these, but if you're like me, roll each one up like a weirdly buttery cigar and chomp at the end of it, savouring the bacon fat running down your wrists.

MUSHROOM, ALE AND LENTIL PIE (VG)

When I first put this down in front of my Scottish Man, he took a bite, then exclaimed immediately how rich it was – which, for the avoidance of any doubt, is a good thing in our house. I then told him it was vegan, and he couldn't quite believe it. Having served this to real vegans on multiple occasions since, they echo his sentiment every time.

These exclamations of disbelief are because this pie rivals its non-vegan counterparts for the presence of a flavour called 'umami', which is a mouth-filling, juicy savouriness. Umami is a phenomenon studied and named fairly recently by Japanese scientists, and it's defined by a high level of a molecule called glutamate. Yes, that's the same one as in monosodium glutamate, otherwise known as MSG. Alongside anchovies and soy sauce, vegetables such as tomatoes, onions, aubergines and mushrooms all hit that famed G-spot (no, not *that* one), so use them where you can to add depth to meat-free dishes. This pie swings on mushrooms and onions as its main sources of umami, plus soy sauce and yeast extract as extra boosters.

You'll need a pie tin able to accommodate all of the filling in a thick layer, or 2–3 smaller ovenproof dishes, if you have something like that.[1] You can also bake it in little ramekins with individual pastry lids on top for extra cuteness – these can be made in advance and frozen before they're baked for a low-effort dinner.

Serves 2–3, takes 50 minutes

YOU'LL NEED:

2 small white onions, or 1 very large one

3 tablespoons of either vegetable or olive oil

a 400g pack of mushrooms

a bunch of fresh thyme, or 2 teaspoons dried

2 tablespoons of dark soy sauce

250ml ale[2]

a tin of green lentils

a tin of borlotti or cannellini beans

a teaspoon of yeast extract (I use Marmite)

300g shop-bought puff pastry (it's usually vegan, but do check)

salt and freshly ground black pepper

OPTIONAL EXTRAS:

a little soy milk, for glazing

steamed broccoli dressed with olive oil and lemon juice, to serve

As usual, start by chopping your onion(s) into rough dice and frying them gently in a frying pan with oil and a little pinch of salt. While they're doing their thing, chop the mushrooms into roughly 1cm dice – you don't want them in slices or big chunks for this. When the onions are translucent, remove them from the pan and set aside on a plate, then add the mushrooms to the pan, along with another splash of oil and the thyme (if you're using fresh thyme, strip the leaves and finely chop them, discarding the stalks). You're aiming to cook most of the water out so you end

---

[1] Disclaimer: this is what I call a weekday pie: one that only has a pastry lid rather than the full long-back-and-sides of a proper pie, which, according to tradition, should have a different pastry on the bottom than on the top. If you want an enclosed pie, there's a recipe on page 123 – or triple the pastry quantity and add 15 minutes to the cooking time if you want to fully enclose this one.

[2] I hate drinking beer, so I actually freeze the rest of it in an old jam jar for next time. There is always a next time with this recipe.

MUSHROOM, ALE AND LENTIL PIE
CONTINUED ←——

up with some browning on the edges of your 'shrooms. After around 10 minutes, or when the mushrooms have some colour on them and the liquid has more or less evaporated, add the soy sauce and some freshly ground black pepper.

Next, add the beer to the pan, then tip in the tin of lentils, followed by the beans – don't bother draining either of them, as the bean-water works well as a thickener. Stir in the yeast extract, then bubble everything on a medium heat for about 10–15 minutes until the alcohol is evaporated and the beer has lost its bitterness. The sauce should thicken up of its own accord here, but if it's looking decided runny after 15 minutes of cooking, then make a paste with a teaspoon of flour mixed with a tablespoon of water, then cook that into the sauce for a further 5 minutes.

While this is happening, preheat the oven to 210°C and roll out the pastry until it's a little thicker than a pound coin.

When you're suitably impressed with the seasoning and texture of your pie filling, scoop it into your dish and pop the pastry lid on top. I've found that tucking the puff pastry down the sides of the filling (as in, *inside* the dish) makes for the easiest, most presentable way of doing things, but if you want to be a bit more artsy and do some crimping or designs around the edge of the dish, then be my guest. Make a slash in the middle of the pastry to allow the steam from the filling to escape, then glaze with a little soy milk, if you like.

Pop in the oven for 20 minutes or so, or until it's puffed up, golden and completely irresistible. Serve with steamed broccoli that's wearing some olive oil and lemon juice.

SAUSAGE, SQUATTERNUT BOSCH AND RED ONION TRAYBAKE (GFO) (VGO)

There was a time when my father would treat me and my brother to a McDonald's Happy Meal every week after swimming lessons. This all changed, however, when Dad started reading books called things like *HOW FAST FOOD DESTROYS EVERYTHING YOU LOVE*. Soon after, the Happy Meals stopped, and instead we trotted home for a filling bowl of organic butternut squash soup and a handful of seeds. While I'll always be grateful for Dad's concern over our health, I'll admit that

as a seven-year-old, going from McNuggets to hot orange purée did take a bit of getting used to. Now, as a grown-up who can appreciate the delicious merits of both fast food and vegetables, butternut squash is on the table without a hint of disappointment. This traybake is a happy meal in a different sense: it requires little washing-up and is an efficient use of your oven if you cook something else alongside it (try the parmigiana on page 61).

Serves 2, takes 45 minutes

YOU'LL NEED:

1 small butternut squash, or half a large one[1]

a teaspoon of dried sage

a teaspoon of dried rosemary

3 medium red onions

a six-pack of sausages, GF if needed (vegan sausages are just dandy here)

salt

vegetable or light olive oil

OPTIONAL EXTRAS:

gravy and mash, couscous or polenta (something splattable, either way), or a virtuous salad, to serve

Preheat the oven to 190°C. Peel your butternut squash and chop into 1-inch cubes (err on the smaller side if you're unsure), then pop onto a wide roasting tin. Drizzle with around a tablespoon of the oil. Scatter over the herbs and ½ teaspoon of salt, then give it a good old shuggle to get everything coated properly and in an even layer. Put this in the oven right now, even if it's not

yet up to temperature, because butternut squash takes the longest time to cook through.[2]

Chop the onions into quarters, making sure their layers don't become too separate. Now you can do a nifty (but optional) trick with the sausages to make them smaller so they cook through quicker and look cute (this only works if you're using pork ones, by the way; vegan or veggie ones probably won't behave in the same manner). All you need to do is pinch the sausage in the middle, then twist one end of it a few times. You can now cut it in half with a pair of kitchen scissors and *voilà*: baby sausages.

When the squash is a little softer around the edges, remove from the oven and add the sausages and red onion to the tray, plus a drizzle more oil, and a grinding of black pepper. Return to the oven for half an hour, shuggling occasionally, until the squash is cooked through, the onions have a slight char on them but give way under a fork, and the sausages are a deep golden brown. If you find everything is going over too quickly, pop a piece of foil on top.

Serve this traybake with gravy and something soft and carby – or, if you're feeling virtuous, put it all in a big bowl with some spinach leaves and bulgur wheat, plus a splash of dressing, and call it a salad.

---

[1] Use the rest in the Roasted Butternut Squash, Peanut Butter and Chilli Soup on page 135.

[2] You can pre-cook the squash chunks (without oil or salt) in a microwave for 10 minutes; that way, everything will roast faster.

HALLOUMI, CHORIZO AND CHICKPEA TRAYBAKE GFO

This is a winner of a dinner; a multicultural mishmash of delicious things that go together very nicely even though they're probably not meant to. If you're using harissa paste for the first time, be careful, as it could be hotter than you think. You *can* do the halloumi all together in the oven with the chorizo, chickpeas and veg, but I like to fry it separately, then plonk it on top, just so it stays dry and crispy.

Serves 2, takes 35–40 minutes

YOU'LL NEED:

½ chorizo ring[1]

a mug of cherry tomatoes, or just any odd ones that need using up

a red pepper

a tin of chickpeas

a tablespoon of harissa paste

vegetable or olive oil

½ block of halloumi[2]

warm pittas, to serve

hummus, to serve

Preheat the oven to 190°C and find a large, deep-sided roasting tin.

Chop your chorizo into cubes (thick-ish rounds are fine, too), then pop into the roasting tin, along with the cherry tomatoes (keep those whole so that the skin chars nicely later on). Chop the red pepper into rough chunks and add that, too.

Drain the chickpeas, and pat dry with some kitchen roll (or something like that), then tip them into the roasting tray as well, along with the harissa paste and a teeny-tiny drizzle of oil.

Mix everything together with a big wooden spoon, so that the harissa paste coats everything. You probably won't need salt, as the chorizo and halloumi will help season the dish, and there may be salt already in the harissa paste. Pop this in the oven for around 25–30 minutes.

When it's at about the 17-minute mark, slice your halloumi however you like and fry it on a medium-high heat until nicely golden all over. This way, everything will be done all together.

When everything's looking dandy, smack it all into some warmed pittas with some hummus and enjoy while marvelling at the centuries of globalisation that have made this dinner physically possible.

[1] Use the rest for the Eggs in Tomato and Red Pepper Sauce (page 49), or for gnawing on as an afternoon enrichment activity.

[2] Use the rest in the Warm Bulgur Wheat, Halloumi and Harissa Salad (page 27).

RED PESTO AND AUBERGINE PASTA VGO

This is the second 'pimp my pesto' recipe in the book, as I understand that for so many people, pesto-pasta forms a bit of a routine staple for dinner. Here's another way to shake it up a bit, which is vegan if you can find a pesto that is made sans cheese.

If you're unsure about aubergine, as I was until the tender age of 19, it's probably because you've not had it cooked nicely. Aubergines, like mushrooms, are fabulous when fried lightly in oil, with enough space around them so that the all-important Maillard reaction can take place, which is what creates the flavoursome browning on the surface

(see page 179 for more detail on browning). Use a big frying pan for this, and fry the aubergine in batches if you have to. Crowding the pan may look more efficient initially, but will only inhibit cooking in the end, as the aubergine will steam rather than fry. Also, if you have the knob-end of a bit of stale, crusty bread that's just going to be chucked away, tear it up and add it to the sauce for the last few minutes of cooking, just like Nonna would do.

This recipe is rather rich and filling, but I'm sure you'll cope.

Serves 2, takes 25–30 minutes

YOU'LL NEED:

a big white onion

a good amount of olive oil

an aubergine

2 portions of dried pasta – any shape you like

a small jar of red pesto – Lidl's own-brand Italian pesto trapanese is vegan

a splash of either red wine vinegar or balsamic

OPTIONAL EXTRAS:

a tablespoon of capers

some fresh basil

a handful of toasted breadcrumbs

Start by dicing your onion and frying it in olive oil in a large, flat-ish frying pan over a medium heat. You *can* skip this step and leave out the onion, but it adds body and depth. Meanwhile, chop the aubergine into roughly 1.5cm cubes. Once the onion is translucent, remove it from the pan and set aside, keeping the pan on the heat.

Start cooking your pasta now, in a large pan of salted boiling water according to the packet instructions, as the rest of the sauce only takes around 10–12 minutes from this point. As soon as your pasta is on, add some more oil to the frying pan, then fry your aubergine chunks, turning them regularly to get them nice and brown on all sides. You can do this in batches, as mentioned above. Add a sprinkle of salt, but bear in mind the saltiness of the pesto later, so don't go overboard.

When the aubergines are lovely, golden and softened, after about 10 minutes, return the onions to the pan and add the pesto, too; tip in the whole jar, then swirl the vinegar around the empty jar to rinse it and loosen the dregs, pouring this in as well to brighten it all up a bit. Let everything meld together, stirring thoroughly for a couple of seconds to get it all homogeneous. If you're using them, stir in the capers now.

Drain the pasta, reserving a smidge of the starchy water to help the sauce stick. Toss the sauce into the pasta pan, along with the basil, if using.

Serve in those plate-bowl thingies if you have them, and top with the optional toasted breadcrumbs.

FRANGLAIS ONION SOUP (VGO)

Bonjour, ma petit noisettes. Le recipe pour onion de soup c'est delicious et very easy. C'est aussi très cheap, avec just cinq ingredients, the bulk of which sont onions et stock. Le only thing that takes temps c'est frying les onions, but c'est well worth it, parce que le caramelisation c'est exquisite et adds so much flavour à la dish. J'aime la soupe avec un giant cheese toastie, mais cheese on toast c'est also parfait.

Je did not take Français in der schule. Désolée.

Serves deux (2) perfectly, takes 1 hour, mostly pour le caramelising à la onions

YOU'LL NEED:

5–6 medium white onions

3 tablespoons of butter, vegan butter or olive oil

a tablespoon of plain flour

a glass of white wine

1 litre beef or vegetable stock

salt

cheese on toast, to serve

OPTIONAL EXTRAS:

a blob of wholegrain mustard

a splash of balsamic vinegar

Slice your onions thinly into half-moons, then heap them all in a big frying pan with either a huge knob of butter, or a big splash of oil if you're keeping it vegan. Add a big pinch of salt. Now, with the heat on medium–low, stir everything continuously. You'll have about an inch-thick layer of onion in the pan, so you'll need to be constantly circulating the layers over themselves to ensure even cooking. If anything's catching on the bottom of the pan, turn the heat down or add a splash of water. You'll stir this slowly for about 15 minutes before you see any hint of colour, but that's OK. This soup takes time and care and love for the first 45 minutes, but then comes together super quickly in the last ten.

So, keep stirring those onions. Hopefully, they'll have cooked down a bit by now, and will be starting to colour. When they're a nice golden brown all the way through, sprinkle over the flour and stir to make sure the strands of onion are evenly coated. Now add the glass of wine, followed by a dash of the stock, keeping everything moving to cook out the flour. Everything should start to thicken up in just a second, so continue to add the stock until the soup reaches roughly the consistency you want (some people prefer it thinner, some prefer it thicker – authentic F.O.S. has no flour but I like mine a bit thicker). Bring to the boil for a minute or two. Taste the soup and think about the balance of flavours. If it needs acidity, I like to stir in a little wholegrain mustard or a splash of balsamic vinegar here, which is incredibly untraditional. If it's too salty, add some more water and live with thinner soup.

Speaking of tradition, the thing you'd usually do here is ladle the soup into bowls, then top with a slice of baguette and a sprinkling of Gruyère before thwacking it under a hot grill for 5 minutes to melt the cheese. However, this makes both the bowl and the soup hotter than Satan's armpits, so I prefer to just make a cheese toastie and dip it in.

Sacré bleu.

VERY SORT-OF AUBERGINE PARMIGIANA (VO) (GF)

Parmigiana, for those of you thus far unenlightened, consists of layers of fried aubergine, rich tomato sauce, mozzarella and lashings of a grated hard cheese, such as Parmesan. These layers are then baked, often with breadcrumbs and herbs on top. All in all, a parmigiana is a little like the outcome you might get if lasagne (page 112) had safe, meat-free sex with moussaka and invited caponata (page 129) to watch. It's also a great recipe for people who usually say they don't like aubergines.

The reason aubergine-haters usually abandon their previously held prejudices when they get a mouthful of this, is that they – the aubergines, not the people – are browned nicely in olive oil, with a good amount of salt, then covered in cheese. Clearly, this dish has no pretences of healthfulness, despite containing two vegetables. My parmigiana has the addition of pesto, because any notion of Italian authenticity can be firmly stuffed into cannoli and dipped in taramasalata.

This dish can be made mostly in a frying pan, and is a great meat-free main to bring hot and bubbling to the table. Choose Parmesan made without calf's rennet if you're feeding proper vegetarians.

Serves 2, takes 35 minutes

YOU'LL NEED:

2 tins of chopped or plum tomatoes

the smallest pinch of sugar

some abstract splodges of pesto (about 2 tablespoons), if you have it lying around

2 lovely, shiny purple aubergines

an absolute shedload of olive oil (do use olive oil here, not vegetable)

a honque of Parmesan or vegetarian Italian-style hard cheese, around the size of a big mouse

2 fresh mozzarella balls

salt

OPTIONAL EXTRAS:

warm bread and crunchy salad, to serve

Make the sauce first, because then it'll simmer happily while you take the time to fondle the aubergines. There are, of course, many different ways to make a tomato sauce, but this is so crude I feel I might be arrested any moment now for suggesting it. Tip both your tins of tomatoes into a small saucepan over a low heat, and add a big pinch of salt, a little pinch of sugar and a tablespoon of the pesto, breaking up the larger tomatoes if you need to. If you want to add a splosh of red wine, or some dried oregano, please don't let me stop you. I've avoided onions and garlic here simply because I don't think it needs it, but feel free to disagree. Taste everything for seasoning, then keep the sauce on a simmer while you deal with your aubergines.

Preheat the oven to 190°C.

Slice your aubergines lengthways into 5mm-thick surfboards, and dust a sprinkling of salt over each slice. I like to slice them thinner than most recipes call for, so they absorb more fat and cook faster. Now, working in batches, fry the aubergine slices in a hefty amount of olive oil in a 20–23cm cast-iron skillet or other Ovenable Pan, until they're browned on both sides. Transfer any cooked slices to a plate, and keep adding olive oil to the pan whenever you feel it's going a bit dry. By the way, if you don't have an Ovenable Pan, just use a normal frying pan, and we'll worry about all that in just a tick.

VERY SORT-OF
AUBERGINE PARMIGIANA
CONTINUED ⟵———

Once you've browned all your aubergines, turn
the heat off everything. If you don't have a pan
that's oven-safe, find a square cake tin or a small
ceramic roasting dish instead. Now, layer the
aubergine slices with the tomato sauce in your
chosen receptacle, spaffing the shaved Parmesan,
torn mozzarella blobs and remaining pesto
between each layer, as if Jackson Pollock was
working with a caprese salad rather than paint.

Top your creation with a final layer of tomato sauce
and some Parmesan (mozz will burn and go too
crispy on top – I mean, if you like that kind of thing,
go for it but I prefer it all gooey inside only), then
bake for about 20 minutes or until proper bubbly
and lush. Common sense would dictate that you
wait for it to cool down before serving, but I like to
give myself minor soft-palate injuries from time to
time, just to keep things fresh.

Serve with hot bread. And you'll want a crunchy
salad with this one, probably.

IMPRESSIVE SHALLOT TARTE TATIN Ⓥ ⓋGO

Tarte tatin comes second only to the Etch-a-Sketch in my list of favourite French inventions, and it's a very close second at that. For the uninitiated, an Etch-a-Sketch operates along the same principles as pineapple upside-down cake, but instead of pineapple rings, it's usually made with thinly sliced apples on the bottom, and instead of cake on top, it's puff pastry.

Oh no wait, that's a tarte tatin, not an Etch-a-Sketch. Sorry.

Tarte tatin is baked with the raw pastry on top, so the idea is that when you invert it, the fruit is all lovely and caramelised, and there's no risk whatsoever of the pastry developing a soggy bottom. It's more of a method than a recipe, really, so you can use any fruit or vegetable you like, within the laws of reason.[1] Scottish Man likes banana tarte tatin, and pineapple works well, too. Here, I'm pushing a really lovely savoury version, as shallots obviously take well to being caramelised, and you can arrange them in a gorgeous pattern, too. If you can only find round shallots, that's legitimately cool – there's no difference in taste at all.[2]

Serves 2, takes 1 hour

YOU'LL NEED:

8–10 longboi shallots

a juicy knob of butter or vegan butter (around 40g)

½ tablespoon of brown sugar

a few sprigs of fresh thyme, leaves picked, or a teaspoon of dried

a tablespoon of balsamic vinegar

a small block of puff pastry (about 200g)

salt

OPTIONAL EXTRAS:

a tasty salad, to serve

Start by getting an ovenproof frying pan, such as a cast-iron skillet, hot on the stove. It should be around 23–25cm in diameter. (If none of your pans are ovenable, do the next few steps as directed in any frying pan you like, and find yourself a large, round cake tin, or a round ceramic dish of the same diameter. Grease it with butter, then set it aside until later.)

Peel, then top and tail your shallots while you heat a knob of butter in the pan. Slice the shallots in half lengthways, then place them all cut-side down in the butter with a sprinkling of salt, arranging them in as nice a pattern as you can manage if you're planning to use the same pan in the oven later. You won't be moving them about much, as you're after a really lovely caramelisation on the cut side, which takes some time. Leave the pan alone with the heat on very low and a lid on (this will help the shallots steam through), and keep yourself amused nearby for about 10 minutes.

---

[1] Do *not* the avocado. Do *not* the tomato. Do *not* the passion fruit.

[2] My own special brain refers to these types of shallots as Spiker and Sponge, referencing the two horrible aunts from Roald Dahl's *James and the Giant Peach*. And, just like the aunts, the difference in their shape seems to have no effect on the temperament of the shallot.

IMPRESSIVE SHALLOT TARTE TATIN CONTINUED ⟵

After that, check to see if you've got some good colouring on the underside of a couple of the shallots, then rotate the pan a bit so the heat distributes evenly if you need to. When the top side of the shallots are feeling a tad softer, remove the lid and sprinkle over your sugar, thyme and balsamic vinegar. Shuggle it all around a bit, then leave for another 5-10 minutes with the lid off.

Preheat the oven to 200°C and roll out your pastry while the shallots continue to slowly cook through. Cut the pastry into a circle the same diameter as your pan.

When you can just pierce the shallots comfortably with a knife, take the pan off the heat. If your pan is non-ovenable, transfer the shallots very carefully – they'll have lost some of their structure as the cellulose has broken down – to your greased tin, arranging them in a nice pattern in there. Drizzle over any buttery, balsamicky juices from the original pan.

Now lay your pastry disc over the top of the shallots, tucking the edges down the sides. Stab the pastry a few times with a fork, then bake for around 20 minutes, or until the pastry is golden brown and well risen. Remove from the oven and leave to cool down for a couple of minutes, then, while it's still very warm, tip the tarte tatin out on to a big plate or chopping board. Don't leave it for too long or allow it to go cold, as it'll stick. I like to eat this with a robust salad full of olives and feta, dressed with balsamic vinegar, to parallel what's in the tart.

SAVOURY EGGY-BREAD-AND-BUTTER-BAKE (VO)

I often raid the reduced sections at supermarkets like some sort of yellow-sticker-obsessed raccoon, sticking my nosy little paws in all the nooks and crannies in order to find a good bargain. Double and single cream are often marked down, which is great for me because I absolutely love the stuff – so much so that I could mainline an entire tub if I was in the mood to render a gaggle of teenagers completely speechless.

Usually, I'll nab a few cheap tubs with the mind to make something sweet that evening or the day after; ice cream, perhaps, or Eton Mess (see page 145). Sometimes though, I forget I've bought it and find it two or three days later, *just* as it's beginning to become socially unacceptable to consume, and has a tiny touch of sourness about it that you wouldn't want hanging about uncooked in a dessert. That's when I'll make this recipe, as usually I've got a stale loaf loitering about, too. And yes, I am wholly aware of sweet bread-and-butter pudding as a concept, and yes, isn't it delicious. The savoury version, however, is new and shiny and fun, so I'm going to play with that instead.

Serves 2 generously, takes 25 minutes

YOU'LL NEED:

a garlic clove

6 eggs

100ml milk

300ml on-the-turn double or single cream (double cream will make it richer)

a teaspoon each of dried sage, thyme and rosemary

any grimy leftover bits of cheeses (if you're vegetarian, check the labels)

½ loaf of stale sourdough or crusty bloomer-type-thing (around 400g)

a tablespoon of softened salted butter

a pinch of salt and some freshly ground black pepper

Preheat the oven to 190°C. Start by halving the garlic clove and running the cut sides around a 20cm square non-stick baking pan (or something of the same capacity), as if the pan were a big metal bruschetta. Use up the garlic properly in another recipe, as it's too strong to use here – we just want a hint of it.

Next, mix your eggs with the milk and cream in the garlic-infused baking pan, then season liberally with black pepper and your herbs, plus a pinch of salt and some hard cheeses, if you have any lying about. This is one of the only times when I'll ask you not to be overzealous with the salt, as you can't really do much to balance it out if you go overboard here.

Now, cut up your loaf of bread into large chunks around the size of a Duplo block and plonk them into the milk-and-cream-and-egg mix. Leave to soak for about 5–10 minutes – depending on how stale the loaf is, you could leave it in there for up to around 15 minutes while you have a shower. Just make sure the chunks don't go so soggy that they disintegrate when you turn them over to thoroughly soak up more of the milk-and-egg juice.

When you're ready to bake, dot little bits of the butter and any leftover cheese in among the bread-crevices, and grind over some more black pepper. Pop it in the oven for 20 minutes until puffy and golden. I would usually say serve it with something green for health reasons, but I have yet to follow my own advice in this case, and enjoy this meal just as it is, in all its crunchy beigeness.

HOW TO COOK VEGETABLES TO GO WITH EVERYTHING (BUT MAKE IT IN THE STYLE OF GEOFFREY CHAUCER)

PROLOGUE

When that April with his showers soote
The drought of March hath demand'd soup
And with the Spring came many roote
And stalk and leafe; and mud to boot
A guide to cook them, I have written.
Forsooth, with Vegetables I'm smitten.

THE BROCCOLI'S TALE

The Broccolie was a strong and fibrous fellow,
A verdaent green; eat by'fore yellow
And he prov-ed well, for he was nutritionally grayte
Providing vitamins K, C, and lash'ed with folate
But popular not, with youngsteres was he
By-cause of the way
This delectable tree
Hath been squish'd and mash'd and boil'd to death:
Too long unto water, he smells of bad-breath
So in-stead of hot water 'neath he shall drop
Try pan-frying quickly, olive oil atop
Or adding in-stead to a mixture of Egges
With smok'd Bacon eke, and a pinch of nutmege.

Study guide: *The author is alluding to pan-frying the broccoli and then drizzling it with olive oil; later in the stanza, they suggest an omelette made with broccoli, smoked bacon and nutmeg. What are the implications of this for the character of Broccoli?*

THE CARROT'S TALE

A Carrote there was and that a worthy man
He is naturally entirely veg'an
Delectably sweet, he loved puréed chickpeas
He has crunch, juice and flavour – but raw,
if you please
Full worthy was he just as he is,
But if thou mus't cooke, bear in your hearts this:
A glaze made of wholegrain mustard and honie,
Or if thou art cheap and desire to save Monie,
A Souppe of Lentils and cumin will do
But the flaevoure of Carrote should always
come through.

Study guide: *The author suggests dipping raw carrots into hummus, roasting them with honey and mustard, or making lentil, cumin and carrot soup. Discuss the relative merit of each suggestion, and its effect on the narrative arc of the stanza.*

THE CABBAGE'S TALE

With Cabbagge there rode some genteele
Seasoning,
Of Butter, black pepper, and of Lemon; a
squeezening
That straight was comen from the wok of Hot
Any other method is worth it not
Unless thou would'st preferen to smell
That old-people, burn'd sock and sulforus hell
That cometh when cabbage is unjystly boyled
No wonder the name of this Goode veg is spoilyed.
(It is to say of cabbage, without any doubte
Thou should'st now treat it the same as a sprout)

Study guide: *The author strongly disagrees with boiling cabbage, preferring it to be stir-fried with butter and black pepper. Are there any adverse childhood experiences in the author's life that may have led them to this conclusion?*

THE MUSHROOM'S TALE

A Mush'roome was there which many afear

But the health benefites of this Fungus are cleare;

Pack'd to the gills with vitamin D

And a goode meaty texture, which some will agree

Lends it self welle to beef Bolognese

Or perhaps even bettere, slic'd lengthwayes

And fryed in the hot spitting fat of a swine

Thenne sprinkled with parsley, on toast; it's divvine.

Study guide: *The author implies that mushrooms can be added to beef Bolognese, but then uses religious language to describe the pleasure of mushrooms fried in bacon fat and sprinkled with parsley. To what extent does the mention of beef foreshadow the reference to pork?*

THE KALE'S TALE

Some Kale there was; a trend, here to stay

It has entice'd younge women

Whom'st've tend'ed to say

That it tastes 'goode' in smoothies

Yet I quoth: 'This be lies!'

Adding Kale to thine smoothie is a heinous disguise

For a pleasant and adequate, mildish taste

Enhanc'd by paprika; or harissa passte

And, in termes of the methode that is bestly deemed

I'd recommende sauté'd, but failing that, steamed.

Study guide: *The author recommends sautéeing kale with smoked paprika or harissa paste rather than blending it into a smoothie. Could the author be jealous of women who drink smoothies? Discuss.*

THE SPINACH'S TALE

Some Spinach there was, of Bottom-Drawer-Fridge

Whose volume, when cook'd, will completely abridge

But alas, fear ye not, for the taste stays the same

And so doth the irone that spinache contain

The best way to cooke it, that I have founde,

Is eating it steamed, with a fork, by the pounde

But Hark!, dear reader, I'm certes enthusiastic

And if thou think'st that Spinach is't not so fantastic

Just wilt it nonchalantly unto soupes, curries, stewe

And soon a love of spinach will growe upon you.

Study guide: *The author makes reference to the fact that spinach shrinks when cooked, and admits to eating it plainly steamed. Is the character of Spinach deliberately diminished by the suggestion of wilting it into other dishes?*

BACKLOGUE

This vegetable pilgrimage is nowise complete

I have not yet discuss'd

Squash, peas, leeks or beets

But take from this anthologie

A TL;DR:

Veggies are wondrous; so make them the star

5 THINGS TO DO WITH BITS OF CHICKEN

I only buy meat when it's got a reduced sticker on it. Certain cuts of chicken, such as thighs, wings and drumsticks, are already half the price of their boneless, skinless, tasteless counterparts, but my reduced-sticker habit makes them even more economical. In the following recipes, you can substitute wings for drumsticks – and, if you really have to, breast meat for thighs. But don't tell me you're doing that, or I'll hiss at you from the bookshelf.

1. I'VE MOZZED YOU UNDER MY SKIN GF

This is a cheeky little dinner idea. Preheat the oven to 190°C. Get yourself a pack of **bone-in, skin-on chicken thighs**, and scoop a teaspoon of **pesto** underneath the skin of each thigh, being careful not to rip it. (Also, DO NOT stick a raw chicken teaspoon back into a full jar of pesto and leave all the salmonella to fester – decant however much you need into a ramekin or mug first.) Slice your **mozzarella ball** and push a slice under each bit of skin, then brush with **olive oil**, and season with **salt** and **black pepper**. Pop onto a lined baking tray and bake for 30–40 minutes, or until the juices of the thighs run clear and there are no pink bits. Serve on a bed of **salady things** with some **balsamic** sprinkled over everything, plus **tatties** or **bread** on the side to soak up the juices.

2. EXTRA LUSH DOUBLE-CHICKEN CURRY GF

I make this using a whole chicken[1] and homemade stock (see opposite), because I am extra, and it makes it like a curry-house version, with lots of flavoursome liquid and honking great bits of meat.

Fry off 3 large **red onions** in an inordinate quantity of **ghee**[2] **or vegetable oil**. Once softened, add a small jar of **tikka paste**, plus 2 finely chopped **red chillies**, 4 minced **garlic cloves**, a teaspoon of **salt** and a grated knob of **ginger**. You then get 6 jointed bits of **chicken** (I use a whole chicken but you can use just thighs and drumsticks if that suits) and plonk them into the pan, stirring it all around. Cover with a litre of **stock** and bring to the boil, then add 3 tins of **chopped tomatoes**. Leave it alone on a medium heat to simmer for around 45 minutes, or until the meat is flaking off the bones a bit. Stir in a couple of spoons of **yogurt** at the end if you need to calm it down. Serve this with lots of **naan**, **Quick Pickled Onions** (page 77) and **Spicy Dicey Spudlings** (page 38).

[1] I'm not expecting you to butcher a chicken but there's a stack of tutorials on YouTube if you fancy a crack at it.

[2] Ghee is butter with the milk solids removed, just to clarify.

3. MEDITERRANEAN CHICKEN STEW WITH OLIVES BUT NOT SUN CREAM GF DF

Gently sauté a small **onion** per person with a couple of **tinned anchovy fillets**, plus a few shakes of **dried thyme**, **oregano** and **basil**. Add a clove or two of finely sliced **garlic** and let it colour very slightly before adding some diced **chicken thighs or breasts**. (100g per person, or roughly one each, is a good estimate, and you can debone your own thighs here if you want to. Not, like, your own, obviously. The chicken ones.) Let them colour a little on the outside before pouring in a can of **chopped** tomatoes plus a small glass of **red wine** for every 2 people. Add a squirt of **tomato purée** if you have some. Bring to the boil for 3–4 minutes, then taste for seasoning and adjust. Cover with something lid-shaped and reduce to a simmer for about 17–20 minutes, adding a mug of **black olives** when you remember them. Stir in a couple of handfuls of **spinach** to wilt just before serving with lots of **crusty bread**, some chopped **fresh basil**, and absolutely no sun cream.

4. SPICY, STICKY CHARRED WINGS GF DF

Get yourself a kilo tray of **chicken wings**, and the biggest mixing bowl you can find. Toss the chicken wings with a couple of teaspoons of **salt**, the grated zest and juice of a **lime**, 2 tablespoons of **runny honey**, a tablespoon of **vegetable oil**, 2 tablespoons of **hot sauce** and a good spronkle of **smoked paprika**. Leave that to sit in the fridge for up to a day if you have the space, or an hour on the counter if you don't. When you're ready to cook, preheat the oven to 200°C and spread out the wings on a baking tray (line it with greaseproof paper for an easy clean-up). Pop them in the oven for about 35 minutes, or until sticky and charred. Finely chop some **coriander** and half a **fresh red chilli** and

scatter over to serve. You can drizzle over a little more honey and some **sea salt** if you like it sweet and spicy. This is mega with some **skinny oven chips**, cooked on the shelf above at the same time.

5. BONE BROTH, LOL GF DF

This nourishing bone broth will alkalise your optimal nerve junctions and reduce inflammation in all six of your adrenal spark plugs. Only kidding – it's just stock. Don't listen to the wellness gurus, because no amount of detoxing will get rid of their bullshit.

Do make your own stock, though; it's great for sauces and stews, and basically anywhere you need to add a quantity of flavoursome liquid that's not wine.

Start by never, ever throwing away **chicken bones**, not even from other people's plates. Set aside a plastic tub or bag in the freezer to store your bones, and when you have roughly 500g, stick them (still frozen) in a big pot with around 2.5 litres of **hot water**, a whole **onion**, a **carrot**, a handful of **black peppercorns** and 2 tablespoons of **salt**. Add any **veg scraps** you have kicking around, such as **carrot tops** or **onion skins**.

Bring everything to a rapid boil for 3 minutes, then keep it bubbling gently for at least 3 hours, making sure the water level remains reasonable – you want to reduce it by about a third over a long time, so top it up if it's going too fast. Taste after about 2½ hours. If it's oversalted, add more water. When it's sufficiently rich and stock-like, strain it through a sieve or a colander and use straight away, or pour into a couple of Tupperwares with good lids and freeze for a rainy day.

N.B. You *can* roast the bones first, but only do so if your oven is already on for something else – it's not worth the energy costs if you're just roasting the bones for stock, even though it does give it a nice, rounded flavour. For bonus points, steam vegetables over the stockpot as it cooks to make use of all that expensive heat going to waste.

CHAPTER 3:
DRUNK

~~~~~~~~~~~~~~~~~~~~~~~~~~~~

From the title, you might think this chapter is going to be all about cocktails and nice drinks recipes. I'm afraid I'm going to have to disappoint you here, because the only thing I know about booze is that I like it. My favourite cocktail is the one that someone else is paying for.

Instead, this chapter draws on knowledge I'm much better qualified to impart. It's all about the food you might eat on the timeline of a good night out. This includes the snackitty-type meal you'd have with pre-drinks (very important), the 'hell-up, I'm starving' 3am food for when you've just got in, and something to return your blood glucose to normal the morning after, if you're able to face anything beyond just water. Perhaps I'm alone in this opinion, but if I'm not feeling too jaded, the morning after feels like the best part of any night out. You know, when you're on the debrief with your pals around the kitchen table, and one of you has just emerged looking like an electrocuted barn owl, and there's a random person there you've met twice who's slept behind the sofa, and you're all telling stories and giggling in disbelief. The only way conceivable way to make this better is with a stack of pancakes, or some hot, buttery rolls in the middle of the table.

Of course, everyone has a different relationship with alcohol, so if you're not a drinker in the slightest, that's literally so fine, and you needn't justify your decisions to anyone. These recipes are still really good if you're on the lime and sodas, and make excellent light dinner options, or, of course, a nicely un-hungover brunch. Chances are, though, if you're young and maybe at uni, alcohol probably lubricates a lot of your night-time socialising. Let the recipes in this chapter cure you of hangovers, and lubricate your daytime socialising too, while saving you money on crap pizza and questionable kebabs.

ACT 1: BEFORE

These recipes are easy to throw together, either for yourself as you sew yourself into your outfit for the night, or for a small bunch of friends if you're hosting pre-drinks. They don't require too much attention, either to eat or cook, and three out of the four of them don't even require a fork if you don't want them to. This is so you can get some food down you and focus your attention on the important things, such as making sure your fancy-dress outfit is the best it can possibly be, and trying desperately to get your spare mate a ticket for the night you've booked. But first...

~~~~~~~~~~~~~~~~~~~~~~~~~~~~~~~~~

... DRINK A GLASS OF WATER VG GF

Let me be mother for a second. Listen to me, sunshine. You start with a glass of water, alright?

Serves 1, takes 1 minute

YOU'LL NEED:

a glass or similar receptacle

a tap that produces water

Take glass to tap. Fill with water. Chug it. Repeat if necessary.

CHEESE, BLACK BEAN AND SALSA TOASTED WRAPS Ⓥ

These are brilliant: full of protein, fibre, fat, and a good amount of carbs to keep you from going too hard, too fast. They take about 3–5 minutes per wrap to cook, as all you're waiting for is the cheese to melt and the beans to heat through. I will say that these aren't the most structurally sound of things to eat cutlery-free, but it can – and has – been done. And do feel free to adjust the quantities as you wish, but don't bother leaving half a tin of beans to fester. Instead, make up the full quantity of beans and keep the rest to add body to a salad, or pop into Smoky Tex-Mex Tomatoes and Beans (page 21).

Serves 4 lightly, takes 10 minutes

YOU'LL NEED:

a tin of black beans in water

a squirt of hot sauce (optional)

a teaspoon of smoked paprika

a teaspoon of ground cumin

a teaspoon of dried oregano

a big pinch of salt

4 large flour tortilla wraps

2 mugs (about 175g) of grated cheese that melts well (Cheddar, mozzarella, edam, etc.)

4 big tablespoons of jarred tomato salsa, or some sort of chutney (use ketchup if you're really desperate)

OPTIONAL EXTRAS:

sliced or mashed avocado

crushed cheesy Doritos

Drain the beans and tip them into a mixing bowl with your hot sauce (if using), smoked paprika, cumin, oregano and salt. Stir everything around, then lightly squish some of the beans with the back of a fork until some are a bit mashed, but don't worry about making the entire thing into paste.

Now heat a large frying pan over a medium–high heat. Once it's hot, throw in a tortilla wrap – you won't need to add any oil here. Sprinkle half a mug of cheese over the whole wrap, then administer your spiced beans evenly on top of the cheese. Dollop around some of the salsa and any other ingredients you fancy (sliced avocado goes well, as do crushed cheesy Doritos). By the time you've spread your beans around, it'll be time to fold the wrap in half, give it a quick flip upside down and then tip it out onto a waiting plate. Crack on with the next one until all the ingredients are used up.

FALAFEL PATTIES AND PITTAS VG

This one is fun, as you can fill the pitta with your falafels and take them with you as you float around the house like some sort of wretched Victorian ghoul in search of something to wear. The falafels can also be made in advance and eaten cold, dipped into hummus, if that's more your style.

This is one of the few recipes in this book that works best if you have some sort of blender. If you don't have something electronical with a blade on the end of it, you can use a potato masher or the back of a fork, but if you're doing that, it's best to add an egg so everything is held together more thoroughly, as you probably won't be able to get it all as smooth as you would by using electricity – and, of course, that means it won't be vegan.

Serves 2 generously, takes 20 minutes

YOU'LL NEED:

For the falafel patties

a small red onion, or ½ medium one[1]

1 phat garlic clove, or 2 small ones

a small bunch of fresh coriander (15–20g or so)

a tin of chickpeas

2–3 heaped teaspoons of plain or wholemeal flour, plus extra for dusting

a teaspoon of ground cumin

½ teaspoon of salt

vegetable oil, for frying

4 lightly toasted pitta breads, to serve

a tub of hummus or some vegan mayo, to serve

something green and leafy (not bamboo), to serve

ketchup or some sort of tangy chutney, to serve

Quick Pickled Onions (optional – see footnote), to serve

Dice the red onion, and grate the garlic cloves on the side of a box grater. Roughly chop the coriander.

Tip everything you've just prepped into a food processor, or into a bowl where you can squish stuff with a stick blender. Now, drain your chickpeas and tip them in, then sprinkle over 2 tablespoons of the flour, followed by the cumin and salt. Pulse everything in bursts until you get a roughish mix which will hold together when shaped – don't overmix it though, or the onion will make everything too wet. If this does happen, don't worry, just add an extra bit of flour and all will be right as rain.

Using a clean pair of hands (which should, for continuity purposes, belong to you), scoop up golf-ball-sized gobs of mixture, roll each into a ball, then squish into inch-thick patties and pop on a lightly floured plate next to the stove.

When you've patted all your patties, wash your hands and heat a generous layer of vegetable oil in a shallow, non-stick frying pan over a medium-high heat. Fry your patties in two batches to avoid crowding the pan, but don't try to lift them or

[1] **Quick Pickled Onions:** If you're using half a larger onion, chop the other half into very thin rings, then pour over just enough white wine vinegar to cover, plus ½ teaspoon of sugar and ½ teaspoon of salt. Leave that for about 25 minutes while you fry your falafels, and you'll end up with some quick pickled onions.

move them until you see the bottom edges begin to colour. This is not the most structurally sound of burger mixes, so be very gentle with them. When the bottom has turned a nice golden brown, after 2–3 minutes, flip them and fry on the other side for a similar length of time. Keep the cooked patties warm on a second plate next to the hob, with some tin foil and a tea towel on top, while you cook the rest.

Stuff the toasted pittas with the falafels and all the assorted 'to serve' items (I really do recommend doing the Quick Pickled Onions in the footnote) and either eat them at the dinner table like a sophisticated person, or drop bits of falafel around the house as you search for that sparkly top you've not seen in months.

FRANKENSTEIN FRIES GF VO

Oven chips didn't really make much sense to me until I realised they're basically another form of nachos, just waiting to be covered with delicious things and whacked under a hot grill. Somewhere around 2015, the restaurant industry realised the same thing, and loaded fries were born. This recipe is a Frankenstein take on loaded fries, in that it uses a load of different stuff you might have in your fridge, but there is one slight difference: I maintain that thicker oven chips are better than skinny ones in this particular context. I love doing these smoked paprika chips with whatever I can find; I love drizzling leftover tubs of ragu (page 126) or some other type of sauce over them, scattering on something like pickled onions or gherkins for extra zesty crunch. Cheese is an absolute must, by the way, for both taste and texture. And to serve it, just dump the trays in the middle of the table and let everyone go bananas.

Serves 6ish, takes 35 minutes

YOU'LL NEED:

1.5kg bag of thick-cut oven chips

2–3 spring onions, or 2–3 tablespoons of baby pickled onions, or 2–3 large gherkins, depending on your preference

2 teaspoons of smoked paprika

a generous teaspoon of salt[1]

½ teaspoon of freshly ground black pepper

a pinch of chilli flakes

2 mugs of grated cheese – basic Cheddar works best here, but low-moisture mozzarella is a close second

OPTIONAL EXTRAS:

These toppings are all optional, but highly recommended. As you can see, anything goes, tbh.

1 measly portion of frozen ragu/tomato sauce/aubergine stew/curry/similar that you decided to keep rather than throw away – and, OH, aren't you just so grateful now?

some ham or cooked bacon or a similar sort of thing – Frankfurters are my favourite, much to the disgust of everyone else around me

more scraps of cheese that really need eating up

the rest of that jar of pesto

hot sauce

anything else conceivably delicious

mayo or sour cream, to serve

leftover tzatziki from that barbecue you had 2 days ago, to serve

more salt, probably, to serve

Method this way ⟶

---

[1] Flaky sea salt is best here if you can find it – and use a bit more of it than you would table salt, as it's not as dense.

FRANKENSTEIN FRIES
CONTINUED ←——

Cook your chips according to the packet instructions, but make sure you're spreading them out over enough trays (two very large ones will do the whole bag for me). This is so they actually crisp up properly. While the chips are in the oven, reheat any of the leftovers you want to use and chop the spring onions/pickled onions/ gherkins into roughish bits. As soon as the chips are done, take them out of the oven and sprinkle them with the smoked paprika, salt, pepper and chilli flakes, then toss around in the trays so that they're all coated evenly.

Preheat the grill. Next, you'll want to sprinkle one of the mugs of cheese over one of the trays of chips, followed by half of the spring onions/pickled onions/gherkins. This is the first place of two to add some of your toppings – try to keep the wetter stuff for the next layer, but here you can sprinkle over any ham, sausage or bacon, plus some of the cheesy bits that will melt nicely. Next, tip your other tray of chips all over the top, spreading them out evenly. Finally, top with the leftovers, the pesto, the hot sauce, Anything Else Conceivably Delicious, plus the rest of the cheese. Thwack that under a hot grill for around 6 minutes until it's properly gooey and bubbling, then artfully drizzle over some extra hot sauce, plus the mayo, tzatziki, and any other condiments you can think of. More is more on this one. And sure, it's not health food, but who's asking?

GNOOEY GNOCCHI WITH PANCETTA, PARMESAN, LEMON AND PARSLEY

This is an absolute winner of a dinner when you're about to go on the lash, as the stodge really does its bit for slowing down your absorption of malicious spirits[1]. It's also great for when you're not out drinking, and just need a bowl of something cuddly, warm, comforting and nice.

Serves 2, takes 10–15 minutes

YOU'LL NEED:

100g pancetta or smoked bacon lardons, or 4 rashers of smoked streaky bacon, chopped

½ lemon

a big thumb-sized wodge (30g or so) of Parmesan or other matured hard cheese, plus extra to serve

a small bunch of parsley

500g pack of gnocchi

salt and a boatload of freshly ground black pepper

Cook the bacon in a frying pan over a medium heat until it's nice and crispy and all the fat has pooled out of it. Zest the lemon, grate the cheese, and chop the parsley very finely – the dish comes together quite quickly at the end, so you can do all this in advance while the bacon is frying.

When the bacon is cooked through but not yet golden, bring a large saucepan of salted water to a rolling boil and add your gnocchi. The gnocchi should float to the surface when they're cooked – this only takes around 3–4 minutes, so watch them like a hawk, as you don't want them to go at all soggy. When they're done, reserve a tiny cup of the starchy water, then drain the gnocchi thoroughly and tip them into the bacon pan (still on the heat). The gnocchi should get a little crispy if you've drained them well enough and your bacon released a load of fat, but don't fuss about it if you're not seeing much colour – it'll still be lovely either way.

Next, add your grated cheese, your lemon zest, the black pepper and the parsley, then add a teaspoon at a time of the starchy water, which will emulsify with the cheese and make a scant but glossy sauce.

Spoon all this into two bowls, and serve with extra cheese and black pepper.

[1] Boo!

ACT II: STRAIGHT AFTER

After you've got home from the club, or the beach, or the park, having danced your little legs off, you should 100 per cent definitely eat something that has some starch in it. I don't know what the physiological magic behind it is, but inhaling something with complex carbs at 3am or 4am makes waking up a few hours later just so much more pleasant. And, of course, you can buy food out in most places,[1] but it's usually another £6–8, and the last time I had 3am fried chicken, it was still frozen in the middle. Did I still eat it? Yes, I did. Would I do it again? No, I would not.

Of course, getting out hot pans and turning on ovens is completely out of the question when you're drunk as a skunk, so the only thing to do here that involves some sort of heating is to make toast. And do have some pre-morning paracetamol and lots of water alongside it. Unlike some of your actions on your night out, you won't regret doing either of these things, I promise.

---

[1] Edinburgh actually has some of the worst options for late-night food in the world; nothing stays open past 3am, and it's all cardboard pizza anyway. I could make a fortune standing on Cowgate with a toaster, some butter and an infinite supply of thick white bread, but then someone might mistake me for being from the Christian Union – which would be a disastrous PR move for God.

GLASS OF WATER, PART II (VG)(GF)

Heller. I'm sum bleddy thirsty. Better drink a big old glass of waterrrrr afore I make me toast.

Serves 1, takes 1 minute

YOU'LL NEED:

a glass

a tap which contains water

some control of your gross motor skills

Find glass from earlier. Take to tap. Fill with water. Chug it. Repeat as neccessary.

THICK WHITE SLICED TOASTIE BREAD AND BUTTER (V)

Serves 1, takes 2 minutes

YOUS'LL NEEDU:

3–4 splices of that toastie extra-thicc bread

a softty block of butterrt

an toaster

Thkjhbads the tost inn the tewyoqter. Makein suen id does'tr burn. Thats;d be TERUBBEL. Sprods the burrert on ttree tost. Musjch it quickliys then dooi it all agosjn unrtyil u are full n need2 go tsleep.

Translation:

Make toast without burning it, add butter and then eat as much as you can before you are full and you need to go to bed.

RECOVERY JUICE VG GF

Serves 1, takes 2 minutes

YOU'LL NEED:

some water, to the tune of 568ml

1 effervescent vitamin tablet, such as Berocca
(orange flavour works best, of course)

2 paracetamols or aspirins, 200mg each

Fill the pint glass with water (use the tap method
on page 74), but don't chug it yet. Drop in the
effervescent vitamin tablet. Pretty bubbles. Watch.
Drink slowly, and carefully wash down the two
paracetamol tablets. Congratulate future self for
waking up with less of a headache.

ACT III: THE MORNING AFTER

OK, so you've woken up. And because you had your dinner before drinking, and then your 3am snackitty snack, followed by your vitamins and paracetamol, you're surprisingly OK this morning. Obviously, not all 12 cylinders are firing as they should be, but with a bit of luck, some caffeine and some more food, you'll be right as rain. You might possibly be quite hungry too, but this, of course, is variable. Therefore, the recipes in this chapter are arranged from most easy to cook and eat with a hangover to least.

∿∿∿∿∿∿∿∿∿∿∿∿∿∿∿∿∿∿∿∿∿∿∿∿∿

GLASS OF WATER (REPRISE) VG GF

Serves 1, takes 1 minute

YOU'LL NEED:

a glass or similar receptacle

a tap that produces water

Tumble out of bed and stumble to the ambition. Pour yourself a glass of kitchen. Wait? What? No, YOU'RE still drunk. Drink the water. Yawn and stretch; determine if there's life.

If so, move on to the next one.

BALSAMIC MUSHROOMS WITH HALLOUMI AND BASIL Ⓥ ⓋⒼⓄ ⒼⒻⓄ

If you're needing more than a glass of water, but can't face the thought of black pudding (see page 93), you might do well with a light and tangy mushroomy brunch recipe. Depending on how up to things you're feeling, you can omit the halloumi and replace the butter with olive oil for a lighter (vegan) take. This recipe serves 2, but feel free to halve it for just you.

Serves 2, takes 20 minutes hungover

YOU'LL NEED:

a 400g pack of mushrooms

olive oil

a nice knob of butter

½ block of halloumi, sliced into 6 or so slabs

a handful of fresh basil

a generous splash of balsamic vinegar (about a tablespoon)

buttered toast, if you want to have it on toast

sea salt and freshly ground black pepper

Slice your 'shrooms relatively thinly (to about the thickness of a pound coin) and, popping the biggest frying pan you have over a low heat, let them colour gently in the olive oil and butter. Grind over some black pepper and a little bit of sea salt.

After about 10 minutes, when the mushrooms are starting to turn nice and golden, push them to the side of the pan and lay in your halloumi slices, adding extra oil if you need. Fry the halloumi for a few minutes on each side or until golden, and

then mix with the mushrooms, while you roughly chop the basil. Add half the basil to the pan and shuggle it all about, adding anything else you like here, really.

When everything's nice and brown, splosh the balsamic vinegar over it all, and then tip it onto some buttered toast. Top with the rest of the basil. If you think it needs more acidity, sploop a wee bit more balsamic over everything.

CHEAT'S OREGANO AND TOMATO BRUSCHETTA (VG)

Using tinned tomatoes is a great way of cheating at breakfast, especially if you're worse for wear. All you have to do is make sure you're reducing them down enough so they're no longer watery, and make sure they're seasoned correctly. They're surprisingly delicious without much else to alter them. If you have any, topping this with fresh basil is a really lovely addition, but really don't worry if you don't.

Serves 2–3 as a light breakfast, takes 15 minutes

YOU'LL NEED:

a tin of chopped tomatoes or peeled plum tomatoes

a tablespoon of soy sauce

a little pinch of sugar

2 teaspoons of dried oregano

a teaspoon of dried basil

a ciabatta loaf, or two little individual ciabattas

a garlic clove

extra virgin olive oil

flaky sea salt and freshly ground black pepper

Open the tin of tomatoes. If you've plumped for plum ones, use a pair of clean kitchen scissors to chop them up inside the tin. Slop into a small saucepan over a low heat and gently simmer the tomatoes with the soy sauce, sugar and herbs while you do your toasts.

Whack the grill on to high, then slice your ciabatta(s) vertically into inch-thick slices. Spread these under the grill and toast them until lightly golden – but watch them like a hawk. As they say, a watched clock never boils, but an unwatched grill *always* burns. Turn them over and do the other side when they're looking gucci. You can also do this in a dry frying pan if you want, but not the toaster; it takes too long between batches and they'll cool down too fast.

When the toasts is dones, halve the garlic clove and rub one side of each toast with the cut sides of the garlic, then drizzle with a smidgen of olive oil.

Spoon the tomato mixture on to the toasts to serve; grind over a little bit of black pepper and some flaky sea salt, then dig in immediately.

RASPBERRY, DARK CHOCOLATE AND YOGURT PANCAKE STACK ⓥ

There's no combination of the above words that *wouldn't* sound good together, if we're being honest. And by the time it's taken you to cook 11 or so pancakes, your hangover should have got a lot better. This pancake stack uses traditional French crêpe-style pancakes, but they're made with self-raising flour for a *tiny* bit of lift. There's nothing stopping you using the American-style fluffy ones here instead – I just prefer the thinner ones.

What you're doing here is basically using the residual heat from the pancakes, in a low oven, to melt the chocolate and keep the raspberries hot. To serve this, I just cut it up into slices, like a cake, and we have as much or as little as we can manage on tender stomachs.

Serves 2–3, takes 25 minutes

YOU'LL NEED:

For the pancakes

110g self-raising flour (a mugful), or plain with ½ teaspoon of baking powder

a tablespoon of sugar

2 large eggs

250ml milk mixed with 50ml water (¾ mug of milk, topped up with tap-juice)

a tablespoon of vegetable oil

a pinch of salt

For the rest

200g frozen raspberries

a tablespoon or two of sugar

100g bar of dark chocolate (the choice of which is completely up to you)

a tub of full-fat, thick, strained Greek yogurt, to serve (plain is fine too)

OPTIONAL EXTRAS:

banana

chopped toasted almonds

Preheat the oven to its lowest setting.

Make the pancake batter by combining the flour and sugar in a large-ish bowl. Make a wee dip in the dry ingredients, and crack the eggs into it. Stir the eggs with a fork or a balloon whisk, gradually pulling in the dry ingredients, until you have a thick batter. If it's too thick to stir, add a splash of the milk mixture. Add the milk and water little by little – you might need more or less than specified, but what you're aiming for is a thinnish batter; thinner than double cream, but not by much. Blend the oil into the batter, mixing well for full emulsification. Add a pinch of salt and put this aside while you zap your razzers.

Put your frozen raspberries into a microwavable bowl or jug with a tablespoon or so of sugar, and zap them for 30 seconds at a time, or until just defrosted. Keep them handy to use later. If you don't have a microwave, put them in a pan on the hob and defrost them with the sugar on a low heat.

Now, roughly chop your chocolate: either use a knife and a chopping board to do it the traditional way, or whack the wrapped bar with a rolling pin if your hungover little ears can take it. Keep this handy too.

RASPBERRY, DARK CHOCOLATE AND YOGURT PANCAKE STACK CONTINUED ⟵————

Start frying your pancakes in a medium-sized, non-stick frying pan over a medium-high heat. Grease the pan with a little smear of vegetable oil after every second or third pancake, and use around a ladleful of batter (50–60ml or so) for each one. They should take a little less than a minute on the first side, and 30 seconds on the other.

When the first pancake is done,[1] tip it onto a large plate and sprinkle over a scant tablespoon of the chopped chocolate pieces, then scatter over a few of the defrosted raspberries (avoid the juice here if you can; just fish the whole raspberries out with a fork). Pop that into the oven while you fry your next pancake, then repeat the process, stacking them on top of each other with chocolate and raspberries between each layer, until all of the pancake batter is used up.

To serve, cut into slices, then spoon over the extra-thick Greek yogurt and drizzle over the remaining raspberry juice. Scatter over any stray chocolate chunks that didn't make it in. You can also slice up a banana and have that with it, too. Chopped toasted almonds will take this to the next level, but that's asking rather a lot of you if you're doing this with a light headache. Have it on me as a suggestion instead.

[1] They often say that the first pancake is a practice one, but that's never stopped me eating it.

ONE-PAN FULL SCOTTISH BREAKFAST MORNING ROLL

Full disclosure: I'm English. This is humiliating for a number of reasons, but mostly because I'd never heard of a morning roll before I moved to Scotland. A morning roll, for those of you who don't know, is a freshly baked white roll found across Scotland, and has god-like status among most of the population. On first inspection, it looks unremarkable; rather like a burger bun that might have seen too much of the inside of an oven. But a Scottish morning roll is much better than any pallid English bap. A proper, bakery-fresh SMR has a crispy yet chewy exterior, but is supremely soft inside, almost pulling apart in cotton-wool-style layers when gently torn into. It is, without a doubt, the perfect vehicle for bacon. But why stop there? Why restrict yourself to one porky product, when three, plus some lamb-offal – otherwise known as haggis – is almost certainly better?

Well, if that sounds like your idea of fun, then let me introduce to you the full Scottish breakfast morning roll. It's exactly what it says it is: a full Scottish breakfast, stuffed inside a morning roll. This is the least dietary-requirement-friendly item in the whole book – possibly in the whole world – so it'd be a bit of a fruitless endeavour to suggest any tweaks that might make things suitable for anyone other than a full, offal-scoffing omnivore. So, if you eat everything, and want to cure your hangover using one pan and most of a pig, then please: be my guest.

Serves 4 generously, takes 25 minutes

YOU'LL NEED:

4 slices of lorne sausage[1]

4 slices of black pudding (I like the Stornoway stuff best)

8 rashers of good back bacon; your choice of smoked or unsmoked

4 slices of haggis

4 tattie scones (potato scones)

4 eggs

4 morning rolls

butter

ketchup or broon sauce

freshly ground black pepper

don't even think about fruit and vegetables, such as mushrooms and tomatoes

Preheat the oven to its lowest setting and line a square roasting tin with foil. You're not cooking anything in here, just keeping it all warm as it comes off the pan.

Find the biggest frying pan you can, and start by cooking the sausage and black pudding together on a medium-high heat, as they're the items most likely to leak an unholy amount of animal fat, which will help flavour everything else as you go. After about 10 minutes, or when the lorne sausage is brown, and the black pudding crispy on the outside and starting to crumble, toss it all into the pre-heated tray in the oven, but keep the majority of the fat in the pan. Next, you'll want to cook your bacon, laying out all 8 rashers in the pan at first, and whacking up the heat so they shrink and start to release their water and fat. When one side is looking cooked and crispy, flip them, and find space to add your haggis slices to the pan. After around 5–7 minutes, when

---

[1] This is a flat, square sausage. It comes in slices off a slab of what looks like pink meatloaf. I have no idea what's in it, and I probably don't want to know, but it's extraordinarily delicious. You can use link-sausages (bangers) instead here, if you must.

everything is a deep golden brown, pop the bacon and haggis into the oven tray too.

Next, you'll want to get your tattie scones out (not a euphemism, but don't let me stop you) and get them in the pan to soak up all those bacon, black pudding, haggis and sausage juices. Fry them until they're crispy and golden brown, then stick them in the oven with the other bits and bobs.

Lastly, you'll want to do your eggs. Crack all of them into the pan, leaving gaps between them, and find something with which to cover everything – a plate, a tray, or perhaps a lid designed for exactly this purpose. Leave over a medium heat for 3–5 minutes, so the whites cook through on top but the yolks stay runny.

Meanwhile, split the morning rolls, being sure to leave a bready hinge still attaching the two halves, and pull out a little of the white middle from the top parts so you have space for everything. Butter the estranged middle parts and eat as a starter while you do the last bits and bobs.

Slice and thickly butter the morning rolls, both top and bottom (yes, I said this was unholy). Check the eggs at this point and take the pan off the hob, to prevent any further cooking.

To assemble the rolls, start with a slice of bacon, followed by a piece of lorne, a black pudding and a tattie scone, then the haggis slice, followed by the second slice of bacon. Slide an egg on top, and, if you're feeling fancy, you can grind a wee bit of black pepper over it. Whether you add sauce is up to you, but I love a wee smidge of ketchup spread on the top of the roll before smashing it down so that the egg yolk spills out of the side.

Eat this with a plate underneath to catch all the bits that will inevitably fall out. My pal likes to heat up some baked beans to dip the roll into, but I think that's a step too far.

And if that doesn't cure your hangover, then there's nothing for it but to go back to bed with the aim of waking up and trying again tomorrow.

5 THINGS TO DO WITH FROZEN PEAS

Frozen peas are just so useful, especially if you're clumsy like me and are prone to needing the occasional instant cold compress. I always have a bag in the freezer, which I use all the time – for both bruises and eating. I prefer the slightly pricier petits pois because they're sweeter and more tender, but obviously normal garden peas are great too. Here are five cute ideas that utilise these marvellous legumes.

1. GIVE PEAS A CHANCE (VGO) (GFO)

It's difficult to think of dishes that aren't improved in some way by peas. Baked Alaska, perhaps. Or spaghetti carbonara. Those two things aside, you should try adding a mug of **peas** to practically everything else. You can bulk up **leftover takeaway curry** with some frozen peas when you reheat it (that's with all the curries mixed in to one Franken-curry, I hope), or scatter a load over **frozen fish parcels** as they bake in the oven. Also primed and ready to swallow a mugful of frozen peas is anything that comes under the category of 'slop' in my brain – that's **soups, stews, casseroles, or anything brown** that needs a hint of healthful green. **Pasta bakes** always do well with some peas thrown in, too, and you can even razz up a quick pesto using cooked peas, **Parmesan** and a splash of good **olive oil**. This goes very nicely round some **spaghetti**, topped with a few **toasted breadcrumbs** for good measure. Gosh, what a lot of ideas. You're so welcome.

2. MICROWAVE MUG SNACC (V) (GF)

This my go-to gremlin snack when I don't have much in the house. What you do is pour yourself a large mug of **frozen peas** and sploosh over a tablespoon or so of water. Microwave that for 2 minutes while you fry an **egg**. Drain any water from the mug of peas, then add a knob of **butter** and a boatload of **black pepper** to them. Tip everything into a bowl and top with the fried egg and some **hot sauce**, and maybe some **peanuts**. Eat it quickly standing up over the sink, you goblin, you.

3. USE AS THE BASE FOR SUMMER SIDE DISHES

Peas make a great addition to summer salads, and you can also serve them – spruced up – at room temperature as a very fancy side dish. Serve the below recipe scattered artfully over a big plate rather than in something as *pedestrian* as a bowl.

Cook a load of **peas**, along with some **asparagus** spears chopped into inch-long sticks. Drain, then spread out on a large plate to cool for a moment.

Grate over the zest of a **lemon**, then squeeze over its juice. Add a handful of finely chopped **mint** and a few thinly sliced **artichoke hearts** from a jar or tin, plus a drizzle of good **extra virgin olive oil**. Toss a little with some **flaky sea salt** if you have it. You can leave this covered for a few hours at room temperature if you're making it in advance, or overnight in the fridge. Serve as a fresh and juicy side to rich and sticky barbecued stuff.

4. MAKE SOME SOUP VGO

Sauté a **white onion** in a generous amount of **butter or olive oil**, then add half a bag of **frozen peas**, plus a litre or so of **stock**. (I boil up ham hocks to make stock for pea soup, because I am actually a time traveller from 1932, but you don't have to – veg stock cubes are just fine here.) Bring everything quickly to the boil, then blend it all together to form a lurid green purée. If you want it thinner, add more water; thicker, add more peas – or some **leftover roast potatoes**. Taste and adjust for seasonage, and add a bit of **lemon juice or white wine vinegar** if it needs to be a bit zippier. Serve it with **crusty white bread**, obviously.

5. BECOME THE LEADER OF AN ARMY OF DUCKS USING JUST A TRAIL OF PEAS, LIKE IN THE FAMOUS FAIRY TALE, HANSEL, GRETEL AND THE MALLARDS VG GF

Once upon a time, a little boy called Hansel went for a wander in the woods with his wee sister, Gretel. Hansel was a smart kid, and so to avoid getting lost, he brought along a bag of **frozen peas** to mark his trail, which was an incredible achievement because the alliterative advancement of field-fresh flash-freezing hadn't even been invented yet.

But about an hour into their walk, Gretel started to notice a strange shuffling sound coming from behind them.

'Hansel! Hansel!' she cried, tugging at his lederhosen. 'Duck!'

And Hansel ducked, but then looked at where she was pointing.

The little boy couldn't believe his optic nerves, for just a few feet behind him was an army of mallards. There must have been at least a hundred of them, beady eyes staring right back at him and his bag of frozen peas.

'Master,' said the leader, stepping forward. (You could tell he was the leader because he was wearing a little hat.) 'Master, you have saved us. Our stomachs were growing sick with only breadcrumbs.' All the other ducks nodded in agreement; a few even quacked.

Hansel stammered and spluttered a bit at this news, but the duck leader continued: 'In return for a daily ration of field-fresh flash-frozen peas, we will form an army to fight off any witches in gingerbread houses who may or may not have cannibalistic intentions towards small children.'

Hansel composed himself (it was a theme tune), then turned to consult with his sister.

'Seems like a fair deal to me,' whispered Gretel. 'I don't want to be eaten by a witch.'

'*Ja*,' agreed Hansel, solemnly. Then he turned to the ducks, and crouched down to address them properly. '*Meine guten Enten*,' he began. 'I will honour my side of the deal. A few bags of field-fresh flash-frozen peas is a petty price to pay for protection against mildly misogynistically framed magical maidens. Please, have some more peas.'

He scattered the peas onto the ground and the ducks happed with quackiness.

'Fantastic news!' said the duck leader, clapping his wings together. 'Now, shall we get back to the cookbook, before our readers think that the author is completely unhinged?'

HOW TO COOK FOR OTHERS WITHOUT IMPLODING IN A BALL OF PURPLE STRESS-RAGE

I mentioned way back in the introduction that you probably have a few friends who let you cook for them now and again. This section is all about how to do exactly that *and* have loads of fun at the same time. There's really no better satisfaction than being surrounded by your pals, squeezed in elbow to elbow, laughter fuelled by the delicious food you've just put in front of them. I would love for you to get as much joy out of feeding people as I do, so this section is dedicated to making things go as smoothly as possible.

MANAGING MONEY

I have a 'the more the merrier' attitude when it comes to friends, so rather than hosting proper dinner parties, which get expensive quickly, I tend to put on what I term 'Nosebag Gatherings'. It doesn't matter whether I'm cooking for six or 16, because everything will be plant-based, plonk-in-the-middle-and-help-yourself food, which helps to keep costs down and also minimises faff around plating. And, unless otherwise stated, it's BYOB, which has the added advantage of people leaving the odds and ends of bottles of wine for me to cook with over the next few days.

At these sorts of events, I think it's absolutely OK to divide up the grocery bill and send everyone a little invoice each. This is sort of an unwritten rule in my circles but if this is the first time you're doing this, then perhaps clarify with your pals that this is what you're up to. The right friends will be very happy to contribute, especially if you've cooked them an enormous feast and worded your message nicely.

If that sounds too awkward, the alternative is to get each person to bring an ingredient or two. When you know what you're going to cook, look at the list and divvy up the ingredients between your pals. This method works until there's more than six or seven of you – any number higher than that and it becomes like herding cats, especially if your friends are perhaps not the most punctual of people and you desperately need the cumin RIGHT NOW. If that's the case, you're better off taking charge of planning and just doing the invoice method.

IT'S POTLUCK, I'M AFRAID

Another way around the budget issue that can be really useful when cooking for groups of more than 12 is to stray into potluck territory. Ask people to contribute any of the following: a nice side dish, a bottle of wine to share, a big loaf of nice bread and some good butter, or a dessert. This means you can afford to cook slightly less of the main course, as there's more of everything else to go round, but do make sure you're being fair with what you're asking people to bring: a not-shit bottle of wine is going to cost more than just bread and hummus. You can also play this game in teams, especially if you're like me and know lots of couples who live together.

Being the control freak that I am, I tend to specify the exact things each person should bring – I'll say red or white wine; a green salad or a caprese salad;[1] enough crisps and dips for 11 of us, etc. In my experience, people tend to like being told what to do, as it gives them a clear sense of direction.

WHAT TO ACTUALLY FEED ALL YOUR FRIENDS

If all your friends eat anything and everything, then you've actually got a harder job, because the world is your lobster – it's down to you alone to decide what to cook, and that can be rather overwhelming. If in doubt, you can't go wrong with a couple of spatchcocked chickens (see page 43), enough potatoes to feed an Idahoan wedding party (check out my ideas on page 38), and a posh green salad.

But if you've got lots of folk to feed, chances are you'll be juggling several different dietary requirements. Contrary to popular belief, I'd argue this actually makes things *easier,* as the best way to manage everyone's needs, including those who are veggie, vegan, lactose-intolerant and gluten-intolerant, is to feed everyone something plant-based and delicious. No quibbles, no debates, no arguments, no stress. Happily, all the meals in the 'Feed your Friends (or Your Freezer)' chapter (which is coming up next, on pages 102–119) swing this way, and all have gluten-free subs, too. Even low-carbers can join in and just avoid the rice or bread being served alongside.

Some concrete plant-based ideas for a slightly smaller crowd include doubling the Mushroom, Ale and Lentil Pie (page 53); making a double batch of the Sicilian-style Aubergine Stew (page 129); or halving any of the recipes from the following chapter. Additionally, the Yellow Split Pea Dal (page 137) ticks almost all the dietary boxes too, as does the Roasted Butternut Squash, Peanut Butter[2]

and Chilli Soup (page 135). Other easy and inclusive dinner ideas are DIY veggie burgers with loads of sides (try my Falafel Patties on page 77 as a base recipe), plant-based risottos, and build-your-own pizza seshes where everyone throws olives at each other and we all have a good time (for a good pizza crust, stretch the Slapdash Bread on page 169 very thinly).

The one thing I'd avoid serving for groups larger than four or five is pasta. For me, pasta *has* to be timed perfectly, so it's ruined if it goes past al-dente stage by a few minutes. This means being tight and strict on dinner timing, and if you've got friends like mine, enforced punctuality is a terrible idea. If your last dying wish is that you want to serve your friends some pasta, make a Massive Vegetarian Lasagne (page 112). It's much more forgiving.

By the way, you should bear in mind that if you're catering for anyone who is allergic to something, such as fish, nuts, eggs or milk, don't even *think* about having these things in the meal plan in the first place. Cross-contamination is a very easy, very dangerous thing to do, and if bad things do happen, it might put you off cooking for a crowd for a long time.

LOGISTICS

So, you've established what to cook. Now, how to go about cooking it.

The first thing you'll want to do is scale up your quantities. Helpfully, I've written an entire chapter

[1] If you know that someone is really good at making a particular recipe, then ask them to bring that; they often love receiving such requests. My most-requested dish for carnivores is my Spatchcocked Chicken (page 43). My pal Wee Laura makes the most delicious vegan banana bread, so I'll always request that if she's coming.

[2] The peanut butter can be replaced with tahini and a pinch of brown sugar, should one of your guests be a Sworn Enemy of the Peanut.

where I've done all this for you over eight or so recipes, but if you're looking to improvise (which I wholeheartedly encourage), remember that more is always better than less – having leftovers is an infinitely more favourable situation than having hungry guests. And if your friends are anything like the lanky gannets I have collected over the years, they'll come back for seconds, and then thirds, and possibly fourths if there are pan-scrapings still to be had, and you'll probably find you won't have to worry about fridge space after all.

The next thing to think about in terms of logistics is worktop space. Many kitchens belonging to those in the 18–25 age group are shared; most are small. If you're cooking for a crowd, make sure you clear the entire kitchen before you start, as things do mount up. With that in mind, make sure you clear as you go, too. This is something I don't often do when I'm just cooking for myself or one other person, but when you're serving a crowd, it makes life so much easier if you have quick three-minute clean-ups every now and again where you put ingredients away or throw stuff into the sink to wash up later.

When it comes to boring or laborious jobs, such as chopping or grating, the more you can delegate, the better, so find yourself some minions. Having an extra pair or two of willing hands means you can offload all the tedious tasks, such as peeling squash or sweet potatoes, while you swan about adding things to the pot and tasting for seasoning like the head chef you know you are. Alternatively, you could do all the prep beforehand yourself, but I think you'll soon realise that it's a lot more fun to get everyone involved and chatting around the table, giving you all time to eat crisps and gossip while building up your appetites.

If you're cooking up a more complicated feast, such as a Sunday roast, you might have to keep things warm out of the oven or off the hob while other things cook through. A handy trick for keeping things toasty is to cover the contents of the tray in foil, then a tea towel, then a normal towel; you'll be able to keep mash, beans and meat warm this way for a surprisingly long time. There are a couple of things you'll want to avoid doing this to, though, and that includes anything with a crispy outside: roast potatoes, pastry, and anything remotely fried.[3] This is because the steam build-up will make everything go soggy under the foil, so just make sure you serve these things straight from the oven or pan. Roasted or seared meats, by the way, should always be rested before serving, so that the meat fibres relax and soak up more of the cooking juices. So if you're resting meat, you can use the method above to keep it warm.[4]

THE SWEETENING

The next secret is pudding. People often don't expect pudding (wrongly, of course, in my house), so when you bring one out, be prepared for people to go mad for it. There's a boatload of good pudding ideas in Chapter 6, obviously, but a thrifty way of making sure most folk are happy is to do a plant-based crumble topping with whatever cheap fruit you can think of underneath (see page 150 for an easy crumble recipe). If you've got gluten-freers *and* vegans, then the Baked Plums in Red Wine

[3] Take the crackling off the roast pork before letting it rest, and keep it in the lowest shelf of the oven to let it get extra crispy.

[4] Of course, this makes roast chicken into something a dilemma, as it has both crispy skin and meat that needs resting. I've always been caught between the desire to rest my chicken properly and the fear of its very crispy skin going soggy, but I've found that a chicken will happily rest for 10 minutes out of the oven without being bundled up, and still be hot enough to serve. And that's partially what lashings of very hot gravy are for, anyway.

(page 147) or the Baked Apricots in White Wine variation (page 148) both go really well with a nice plant-based vanilla ice cream or custard. If you've thought ahead, then doing coconut-cream ganache pots is a sure-fire way to keep literally *everyone* – including low-carbers who generally can't eat much pudding - happy as Larry. Just heat up a tin of **coconut milk** until simmering, pour it over 200g of chopped 70 per cent **dark chocolate**, and stir gently together with a teaspoon of **vanilla extract**. Pour this into six ramekins, top with a few artisanal bespoke decadent luxury flakes of **sea salt** and set in the fridge for an hour or so.

someone like me who is *very* practised at feeding large crowds. Just make sure someone else has laid the table, and that you sit on the chair closest to the kitchen for when you remember the peas sitting in the microwave.

Lastly – and I should take some of my own advice more often with this one – when people compliment your food, be sodding gracious about it rather than picking holes and telling them everything that went wrong when you were making it.

Oh, and chefs eat last, by the way. Them's the rules.

THE AFTERMATH

You've just cooked everyone a big feast, so you can put up your feet, enjoy a glass of wine and pick at the crumbs from the cake plate while everyone else does some tidying up. If you're lucky enough to have a dishwasher, then count your blessings.

SOME GENERAL ADVICE

Your friends are your friends for a good reason: they will help you if you need it, and if anything goes a bit wrong, they really won't mind. Don't get too frustrated about things being late or slightly misshapen, either; most people are just happy that someone else is cooking for them. Perfection is a stupid thing to try to achieve with group meals, and even if you do absolutely nail something, people probably won't notice, as they'll be too busy chatting. It's only food, after all.

The moment just before serving a big group meal usually gets a little frantic with all the timings coming to a head, but this is normal, even for

CHAPTER 4:
FEED YOUR FRIENDS (OR YOUR FREEZER)

~~~~~~~~~~~~~~~~~~~~~~~~~~~~~~~~~~~

Being a young person, in my experience, is mostly about socialising and having no money. To that end, then, this chapter is dedicated to feeding around eight people at a time, while on a relatively tight budget. If you've not read the previous section on how to cook for lots of people without turning into a giant ball of purple rage, do give it a skim for some hints about how to make it all go smoothly, and how to ask your friends to bank transfer you some cash without seeming tighter than two coats of paint. You can very much double the recipes here if you want to feed even more, but cooking times will go up, so you'll have to instruct everyone to drink more wine and eat more crisps while they wait.

Alternatively, if you don't have any friends, this chapter is a winner for batch-cooking ideas. Simply portion up in those little takeaway containers you seem to have accumulated, and freeze, ready to defrost at your leisure. Everything works well from frozen except the pavlova, which you're probably not going to make for just yourself. But don't let me stop you if you reckon you can manage ten portions in one go. In fact, I'll be mightily impressed if you can eat ten portions of pavlova. Of course, if you just want a few servings of anything in this chapter, halve or quarter the recipes and adjust the cooking times accordingly.

The dishes in here are all vegan or veggie, because it keeps costs down and everyone can eat the same thing without having to faff too much[1] with extra dishes – that's all explained on page 98, of course. I've also made sure there are at least two recipes that are not only vegan, but gluten-free, too, due to my rule that everyone must be able to at least eat the same main course; a rule that I obviously break moments into the lasagne recipe. And I know that the ingredient lists can seem long at times here, but it's mostly aromatic ingredients (ginger, garlic, chillies, etc.) and spices that are taking up the space. I've also been very thorough with the method, hence why it seems quite wordy in places. You'll get around this, I'm sure, and end up cooking fabulous meals for all your weird and wonderful friends.

And do enjoy the Dustbin Punch recipe on page 117. It's a belter.

---

[1] If you are feeding six or so carnivores, turn to Spatchcocked Chicken in the Dead of Night (page 43) and cook three of them rather than one, or triple the Spicy Sticky Charred Wings (page 71). Either way, put everything in the middle of the table with a phat bunch of oven chips, lime wedges, salad and some dips, and let everyone go mad.

FRAGRANT VEGETABLE CURRY WITH COCONUT RICE VG GFO

This is a lovely change from the usual heaviness of group meals; it's fresh, spicy and fragrant, as well as being just a little bit healthy with all that veg involved. Rice is one of those things I'm not well versed in cooking, but this coconut rice is delicious and relatively difficult to mess up. It'll make more than you actually need, but it's so nice that you'll probably eat more than you actually need. The curry freezes well if you're batch cooking, but make the rice fresh each time for food safety purposes.

This is inspired by Thai green curry, but the astute reader will have noticed that I'm about as Thai as a tin of baked beans; accordingly, anyone who knows about South East Asian cookery will immediately spot that the curry is missing two of the usual ingredients: fish sauce (*nam pla*) and lemongrass (*takhir*). This is because you can't get lemongrass at Lidl, and fish sauce isn't vegan. If you have the ability to use both here, please, please do, and sub the soy sauce for shrimp paste, too. Likewise, if you can find galangal root and lime leaves, do use them instead of ginger and lime zest as specified in the recipe below. Or cheat and use shop-bought paste that has those ingredients in it. I won't mind. Really.

Serves 6–8, takes 40 minutes

YOU'LL NEED:

For the paste:

a big chunk of ginger (30–40g)

5 garlic cloves

5 green finger chillies (fewer if you're soft, more if you're hard)

zest and juice of a large lime

a packet of fresh coriander (40g), or all the leaves and stalks from a windowsill supermarket plant

a packet of fresh basil (40g), or, if you have access to Thai basil, 40g of that

5 tablespoons of soy sauce (find a GF one if you've got a glut of coeliacs)

½ teaspoon of salt or MSG[1]

For the rest

a whole bunch of spring onions

6 pak choi (or, if that's over budget, ½ large white cabbage and a 250g bag of spinach)

4–5 peppers, your choice of colour

2–3 tablespoons of vegetable oil or coconut oil

200g cashew nuts

400ml vegetable stock

2 tins of full-fat coconut milk

2 tablespoons of soft dark brown sugar

2 packets of sugar snap peas (use 2 mugs of frozen green beans for a budget version)

2 mugs of frozen peas

a fresh red chilli

200g peanuts

For the rice

500g (3 full-to-the-brim mugs) white long-grain rice

a tin of coconut milk

a pinch of salt

a teaspoon of sugar

[1] Uncle Roger is watching me; I can feel it.

To make the paste, put all the ingredients in a blender and whizz together. If you don't have that option, pound it all in a pestle and mortar, or simply grate the ginger, garlic, chilli and lime zest on the fine bit of a cheese grater, then chop the herbs as finely as possible, and mash it all together in a bowl with the lime juice, soy sauce and salt.

Next, make the rice. It will take a while to cook because of the quantity, so if you start it now, it should be done at the same time as the curry. Rinse the rice until the water runs clear to get rid of any starch, then put it in a large saucepan with the coconut milk and two mugs of cold water, plus the salt and sugar. (If the coconut milk has separated, scoop the fat into a microwavable bowl and zap for 30 seconds to melt it again before pouring over the rice. If you don't have a microwave, then melt the fat in a separate pan over a low heat.) Give everything a quick stir, then pop over a low heat and cook gently with the lid on for 20–25 minutes, without stirring it at all. This will then sit happily with the heat off until you're ready to serve it, should your chopping take longer than expected.

Back to the curry. Top and tail the spring onions and separate the white bits from the green tops. Finely slice the white bits into rings, then do the same with the green bits, but set them aside for later. Separate the leaves from the bases of the pak choi, slicing the white bulky bits into inch-long pieces. Set aside the leaves for later, too. If you're using cabbage instead, slice it very thinly. Thinly slice your peppers.

Get a wok or a big frying pan hot and glug in the vegetable oil. Pop in the white bits of the spring onions, followed by the green curry paste, and fry that off until it's fragrant. Next, add the cashews and stir so they get nice and coated with the paste. Now add the vegetable stock, followed by the white parts of the pak choi (or the cabbage, if you're using it). Stir well, then add your tins of coconut milk and the brown sugar. Bring this to the boil for a good 10 minutes, then add your peppers and sugar snaps/green beans. Cook for another 5–7 minutes, then add your frozen peas and pak choi leaves (or spinach, if you're using it).

Finely dice the red chilli and roughly chop the peanuts. Put them both in little dishes on the table, along with a bottle of soy sauce. Taste the curry for seasoning, then serve with a big ladle in the middle of the table.[2]

Fluff up the rice and let everyone dig in, sprinkling the peanuts and chilli over the curry for a bit of added texture and colour. Use bowls for this, not plates, as it's meant to be relatively runny.

[2] You can cool it down with plain yogurt or dilute with some more stock if it's a bit too spicy.

SWEET POTATO, SPINACH AND CHICKPEA CURRY VG GF

This curry will feed veggies, vegans and gluten-free-ers generously and cheaply, plus you can get the hands-on time down to about 20 minutes if you're fast at chopping onions and have a sharp veg peeler. Should you be such a legend as to own a pestle and mortar *and* a selection of whole cumin, fenugreek, coriander and star anise, please do toast them and grind them up to use in this recipe. But I understand that's not in everyone's skill-basket, so I've included the ready-ground options here, which you 'bloom' in the oil before adding the onions. It's all reinforced with a jar of spice paste, for back-up.

If you are indeed feeding the 5,000 rather than just the freezer, the secret to making this dinner as fun as possible is to have all the trimmings to go along with it. So, cook a vat of rice and get people to bring one accompaniment each to share around – poppadoms, naans, rotis, mango chutney, raita, lime pickle, and Quick Pickled Onions (page 77). I know they're not all meant to go together, and you don't need all of them, by any means, but it's great fun to have a vast selection of condiments and side dishes covering the table. It also means you'll have a huge feast and no one will go hungry, which is always my biggest fear.

The quantity of food below will probably give you leftovers unless you're feeding athletes, but it's even better the next day after sitting in the fridge for a bit.

Serves roughly 8, takes just over 1 hour

YOU'LL NEED:

3 huge sweet potatoes (around 1.5kg altogether)

4 medium red onions

vegetable oil

2–3 fresh red chillies, or a scant teaspoon of chilli flakes

a big knob of ginger, about the size of an espresso cup

5 garlic cloves

a tablespoon of ground cumin

a teaspoon of ground turmeric

a teaspoon of ground coriander

a tablespoon of garam masala (failing that, a teaspoon of ground cinnamon)

a jar of Indian-style curry paste[1] at your preferred spice level

4 tins of chopped tomatoes

2 tins of full-fat coconut milk

4 tins of chickpeas

a 450g bag of fresh spinach, or 200g frozen spinach

salt, to taste

fresh coriander leaves, to serve

Start by chopping your veg. Peel the sweet potatoes, then cut into 1-inch chunks. If you're pushed for time and want this curry on the table ASAP, you can microwave the chunks in batches, covered, for 10 minutes at a time while you chop your onions. If you're more chilled on the

---

[1] Make sure you buy paste, not sauce. They're very different things, so check the label before you put it in your basket. Sauce jars are bigger and watery and grim; paste jars are smaller and oily and great.

timescale, then don't worry; they'll cook through in about 35-40 minutes in the pot.

Speaking of pots, find a really big pot. No, bigger than that. Yes, that one. Chop your onions into half-moon slices while you get a generous amount of oil hot in the bottom of this gigantic pan on medium-high. Finely chop your fresh chilli, if you're using it, then grate your ginger and garlic on the fine side of a cheese grater.

Add your ground spices to the hot oil in the pan, and let them cook until they're nice and fragrant. Then, add your chilli, garlic and ginger, and stir that around before adding the jar of curry paste. Cook for a minute, then, when that's all looking beautiful, add your onions and reduce the heat to low, popping a lid on the pan while you do a light touch of tidying for 10 minutes.

Next, add the sweet potato chunks, followed by the tinned tomatoes. Stir all this around a bit and increase heat to medium-high. Bring to the boil before adding your coconut milk. Bubble for a good 20 minutes to reduce, then taste for seasoning. Drain your chickpeas[2] and stir them through to soak up the flavoursomeness for the last 20 minutes of cooking. If you're using frozen spinach, add it now, but if you're using fresh, wait until just before serving before adding it in handfuls and letting it wilt down – don't try to put the lot in in one go, because it just won't fit. The curry is ready when it's sufficiently thickened and the sweet potatoes are properly cooked through. Serve with all the appropriate bling, plus the coriander leaves roughly chopped and scattered over the top.

[2] The liquid from a tin of chickpeas is called aquafaba, and can be used as a replacement for egg whites to make a vegan version of the pavlova on page 115. Visit www.cookveggielicious.com for a great, very detailed tutorial that shows you how to do this; it's not quite as simple as a 1:1 replacement.

RICH ROOT VEG STEW VGO GFO

Should you ever need to cook veg stew and mash in the middle of nowhere without any electricity or running water, to feed 45 very hungry people after they'd been up some big hills, here's exactly how you'd do it. And yeah, sure this recipe makes 30kg of stew, but what of it?

Impractical? What do you mean, impractical? It was actually very practical when I managed to feed the entirety of Edinburgh University Mountaineering Club for about nine pence each.

Urgh, fine, if you want to make it for a smaller crowd of around eight, I've provided alternative measurements, but I've also included the original massive quantities on the next page. The method is the same.

You could make this gluten-free by omitting the beer and yeast extract; if you do so, replace with more wine and some gluten-free soy sauce.

Feeds 8–45, takes 1.5–2 hours

TO FEED 8

YOU'LL NEED:

For the stew

1 small swede (500g when peeled)

6 large parsnips (500g)

6 large carrots (500g)

3–4 tablespoons of vegetable oil

4 white onions

a sprig or two each of sage, rosemary and thyme, plus extra thyme sprigs to serve (optional)

250ml white wine

a tablespoon of wholegrain mustard

a tablespoon of yeast extract (I use Marmite)

about 1.5 litres vegetable stock

200ml stout[1]

a small bag of baby potatoes (250g)

a tin of cooked green lentils

a mountain of freshly ground black pepper

a teaspoon of salt

For the mash

use the Creamy Dreamy Mishmash recipe on page 39 (use plant-based butter and milk to make it vegan)

Right. Get some minions to chop all your root veg (swede, parsnips, carrots) into even chunks, probably about the size of those large Duplo blocks – you're gonna be stewing this for a long time, so you want it to cook well and be tender without falling to bits. The only thing I bother peeling is the swedes – and the onions, obvs.

Put the oil into a large saucepan and heat that up over a medium heat while you dice your onions.

By the time you've chopped them, your pan should be more than ready to take them, and will sizzle-bizzle like mad. Add salt and pepper and your woody herbs immediately, then pop the lid on to make the onions sweat for about 20 minutes, or until they are translucent. Now, add all your chopped veg – forget about the spuds for a while, we'll deal with them later – and stir it around for a wee bit before glugging in that £4.50 Pinot, in addition to the mustard and yeast extract. Cover with the lid again and simmer for a wee bit, just to get the veg nice and flavour-infused.

---

[1] Use the rest in Beef and Stout Stew-pie on page 123, or make Nigella's stupidly delicious Chocolate Guinness Cake at www.nigella.com

RICH ROOT VEG STEW
CONTINUED ←———

Now, you can add your stock. The quantity should just cover the veg (when I first made this, I just sloshed in cold river water until I felt like it was enough, then threw in a packet of stock cubes – unwrapped of course). Then, you can let that sit on a medium heat for about 40 minutes (2 hours if you're doing the massive version below) with the lid off, while you have a stupidly long shower, watch something daft on YouTube or do some life admin, or ladmin, as I affectionately term it.

Ladmin complete, you can check the stew again and add the stout just as the veg is getting soft. Now, you can toss in a whole bag of baby potatoes without doing anything to them if they're small; just chop them in half if they're a bit bigger. Also, take the time to taste the stew at this point – does it need more salt? More pepper? More yeast extract? Ultimately, you're on the home run now, so you can cook the stew until all the veg and spuds are tender. I like to do all this about 4 hours before serving, because then you can turn off the heat and leave it so that all the flavours get a chance to get to know each other and meld together. This'll also give you some time to make the mash.

About 10–20 minutes before serving, put the stew back over a high heat and add your lentils, which will thicken things considerably if you drain them, but will keep roughly the same viscosity if you don't. Make sure everything is really hot, then scatter over extra sprigs of thyme, if you like, before serving with the creamy mashed potatoes. Sorted.

TO FEED 45

Simply up the quantities to the below and make sure you have an industrial-sized saucepan (honestly, you could charge £450 pcm rent for the one I used if it were centrally located).

YOU'LL NEED:

3 large swedes

3kg parsnips

4kg carrots

300ml veg oil

2.5kg onions, half red, half white, or whatever – doesn't matter

more sage, rosemary and thyme than Simon and Garfunkel anticipated on their trip to Scarborough Fair

1 bottle of white wine

most of a jar of wholegrain mustard

a quarter of a jar of yeast extract (I use Marmite)

about 6 litres vegetable stock

a 500ml bottle of stout

2.5kg bébé potatoes

6 tins of cooked green lentils

a mountain of freshly ground black pepper

a tablespoon of salt

For the monster mash (use the method on page 39)

7.5kg sack of white potatoes

1 litre milk (use soy milk to make it vegan)

2 pats of butter or vegan butter

salt

MASSIVE VEGETARIAN LASAGNE

I make this periodically when I have a big crowd to feed, using yeast extract and soy sauce to add depth. It does take a wee while to make, but it's worth it – plus you can do everything in advance and then assemble when you like. This lasagne also errs on the sloppy side, rather than being one that you can cut into distinct squares, but I prefer it that way.

The bechamel (white sauce) here is a proper one, too, as opposed to using plain ricotta as some recipes suggest.[1] It's loaded with nutmeg and strong Cheddar cheese for the best hallucinogenic-dream combination possible. The secret to a good, smooth white sauce, by the way, is adequately cooking the flour so that the starch grains burst and form a gel with the liquid. The practical way to achieve this is by cooking out the flour and butter

for longer than expected, then adding your milk in tiny little increments. If you've not made a white sauce before, don't worry – it's not difficult. Keep everything gentle, but if it does go lumpy, just blend it and add it back to the pan.

To make this completely animal-free, you can make the sauce with unsweetened soy milk and vegan butter, plus some nutritional yeast and a boatload of dried herbs. I have done small batches of that and made little baby lasagnes alongside the veggie one for my plant-based pals. It breaks my rule of 'everyone eats the same thing' but I can't fathom lasagne without cheese, even though the vegan version is still perfectly delicious.

Serves 8 generously, takes 2½ hours

YOU'LL NEED:

a 500g box of lasagne sheets

For the red sauce (I can't call it ragu or Nonna will throw things):

5 small brown onions, or 3 big ones

3 medium carrots

2 large celery stalks (optional)

olive oil

a heaped teaspoon of dried basil

a heaped teaspoon of dried oregano

650g mushrooms (a family pack)

½ tube of concentrated tomato purée

200g dried red lentils

3 tins of chopped tomatoes

2 very large glasses of red wine

3 tablespoons of soy sauce

a tablespoon of yeast extract (I use Marmite)

salt and freshly ground black pepper

For the bechamel:

a 250g block of extra-mature Cheddar

just under ½ block of butter (100g)

¾ mug of plain flour (100g)

1 litre milk (I use UHT semi-skimmed milk because it's cheaper and keeps in the cupboard)

a mouse-sized (25g) chunk of Parmesan or vegetarian Italian-style hard cheese

fresh nutmeg ready to grate, or a teaspoon of dried nutmeg

OPTIONAL EXTRAS:

mustard (Dijon, wholegrain or English is fine)

steamed spring greens or broccoli

garlic bread

[1] My mother had an awful habit of using yogurt in place of the bechamel or ricotta, which I do not recommend on any terms. Sorry, Mum.

Start by making the red sauce, as it's the most forgiving in terms of time and prep. Finely chop your onions, carrots and celery (if using) into tiny little dice while you heat a thin layer of olive oil in the bottom of a big vat-style saucepan. Add the onions, carrots and celery to the pan, along with ½ teaspoon of salt, the pepper and all your herbs. Fry this mixture gently, covered with a lid.[2]

While that's softening, roughly chop the mushrooms into approximately 2cm dice. When the onions, celery and carrots are soft, add the tomato purée followed by the mushrooms, then stir to combine. Cook for about 5 minutes, then turn the heat up a notch or two and add your lentils, followed by your tinned tomatoes and your wine.[3] Now add your soy sauce and yeast extract, and give everything a good stir before leaving it to bubble away on a medium heat while you make the bechamel, remembering to stir it periodically.

To make the bechamel, firstly grate the Cheddar, reserving a mug's worth or so for sprinkling on the top later. Then, melt the butter in a large, heavy-based saucepan over a low heat. Add the flour and stir until you get a paste. Using a wooden spoon, beat the flour and butter against the sides of the saucepan for about a minute, then add a dash of milk and switch to a balloon whisk if you have one (stick with the spoon if not). Continue whisking on a gentle heat and adding dashes of milk, a little at time, making sure the paste is very smooth after each addition. You can make your dashes longer as you go, but the aim is to not have any lumps at all, so if you end up with some, just continue stirring vigorously and cooking until they're gone, before adding the next splash of milk. When all the milk

is used up, you should have a runny sauce, but don't worry; it'll thicken up as the starch grains continue to cook.

Keep stirring the sauce until it's the texture of custard, then add the Cheddar, reserving a little to top the lasagne. Grate in the Parmesan and add your nutmeg – go mad with it. Stir until the cheese has melted, then taste. Does it need salt? Probably not at this point. You're welcome to add a teaspoon of mustard in here if you like, by the way. Turn off the heat if you're happy with the sauce, and start assembling your lasagne.

Preheat the oven to 190°C as you start the assembly – it'll probably be up to temperature by the time you're ready.

Layer a ladleful of red sauce into the bottom of a big, deep roasting tin or a couple of rectangular ceramic dishes, then shuggle it about to make an even layer. Pour a thick zigzag of bechamel over this, then top with a layer of lasagne sheets. I've never found a tray that houses a perfectly round number of lasagne sheets, so play pasta-Tetris and break bits up until you have an even layer. Repeat this process until your tray(s) are full and your sauces are used up, making sure your final layer is bechamel. Top with a sprinkle of that cheese you reserved earlier.

Bake for around 45 minutes, or until bubbling and golden. Leave to rest in the tray for at least 10 minutes before serving, as oh, BOY, this gets hot. I like serving this with heaps of steamed spring greens or broccoli, plus a cheeky side of garlic bread, popped in the oven as the giant slabs of lasagne are resting.

---

[2] You're making what the Italians call *sofrito*, and the French call *mirepoix* (OK, granted, there's some nuance in the ratios). Essentially, it's a base of carrots, onions and celery that adds depth to final dishes. I've left celery as optional, as it's annoying to have hanging around if you don't actually like eating it raw, so only buy it if you'll use it up.

[3] Top tip: add the wine using the tomato tins, swirling as you go to get all the bits out.

FRUITY PAVLOVA (V) (GF) (DFO)

Look, I like pudding. You'll see real evidence for that when you reach the desserts chapter. But doing sweet stuff for a really big crowd can often be quite expensive as ingredients like fresh berries, high-quality dark chocolate and mascarpone can add up quickly.

This is where the genius of eggs comes in. They're pretty cheap, and if you whip up eight egg whites with a wee bit (ok, half a kilo) of sugar, you can make a crispy but marshmallowy pavlova base on which you can spread 300ml lightly whipped double cream, followed by whatever fruit is on offer at the supermarket. It honestly doesn't matter with pavlova – anything (except maybe tomatoes) is fair game. Kiwis and strawberries are really good, but if you wanted to play it super cheap and mix up your desserts, you could use sliced bananas and then drizzle the whole thing with chocolate or caramel sauce meant for ice cream. Or do a classic zap of Ye Olde Frozen Berries in the microwave with a little bit of sugar or honey.

It's best if you make the pavlova base a few hours – or even a day – ahead, to give it plenty of time to firm up outside of the oven. I make it in the evening, then leave the oven door open a bit overnight for it to cool down, before putting it in a big airtight biscuit box to stay crisp. And don't whinge at me about not having an electric whisk. I don't have one either. Use your triceps, or borrow someone else's if you're being smart about things.

Serves 8–10, takes around 2 hours plus cooling

YOU'LL NEED:

8 egg whites[1]

2 teaspoons of cornflour (not essential, but useful for texture)

500g caster sugar

2 teaspoons of white wine vinegar or lemon juice (again, not essential, but useful for texture)

a pinch of salt

For the filling

300ml double cream, possibly mixed with some Greek-style yogurt or crème fraîche if you want to make it go further (Oatly do a whippable oat cream if you want to keep this dairy-free)

see above for ideas, but otherwise, a 300g bag of mixed frozen berries if you're keeping costs low

a couple of tablespoons of caster sugar, to taste

Preheat the oven to 130°C, going a bit lower if your oven tends to run hot. This needs to bake slowly and uninterrupted, so make sure no one else wants to use the oven in the next few hours, because it'll be ruined if they do. This is a selfish pavlova – at least during the beginning stages. Line a large baking tray with greaseproof paper.

Whip up your egg whites until they form stiff peaks (hold the bowl upside down over someone's head for a laugh) then whisk in the cornflour and salt, followed by the caster sugar, adding it a couple of spoonfuls at a time and beating after each addition so that the mixture goes thick and glossy. This will take literally forever, but it's quite fun to watch the egg whites change shape, so stick with it. Whisk in the vinegar or lemon juice, then spread out the meringue mixture on the prepared tray until it's about 6cm deep and the size of a large serving plate, with a bit of a crater in the middle.

[1] See page 175 for a bonus yolk use-up recipe. Otherwise, use them up in my Savoury Eggy-bread-and-butter Bake (page 67), substituting two yolks for one egg.

FRUITY PAVLOVA
CONTINUED ←

Bake for 1½ hours, but if it looks like it's colouring too deeply, turn the heat down and cook for longer. When it's done, and dry to the touch, crack open the oven door and leave it to cool slowly for a few hours, or overnight.[2]

To assemble the pavlova, find another pair of triceps and lightly whip the cream until it's spreadable. Add any extra yogurt or crème fraîche in here if you want. You can sweeten the cream with a little icing sugar or honey before whipping.

Toppings-wise, if you've gone for the frozen-fruit option, zap the berries in a big bowl in the microwave for 3 minutes, along with a few tablespoons of sugar, then let that cool for a few moments as you transfer the pavlova to a plate and spread it with the whipped cream. (Alternatively, pop the berries into a pan with the sugar and leave to bubble until the sugar has dissolved and the berries have burst.)

When you're ready to serve, spoon over the cooled berries, keeping back some of the juice so it doesn't dissolve the meringue, or top with any other fruit you fancy using. Serve with a flourish, and await the silence that comes only when people are *really* enjoying their food.

Do *not* try to transport this anywhere, by the way, except from the kitchen to the dining table. Just don't. Especially not on a bicycle. Really, please take that one from me. Make the Eton Mess on page 145 if you want a meringue-based dessert that can travel.

[2] Do not, under any circumstances, forget about it in the oven and whack it up to 230°C to make oven chips without remembering to take it out first. That'd be silly.

DUSTBIN PUNCH

For legal reasons, this serves 3,000 people

Firstly, plan a big party and invite literally everyone you know, plus a few more you don't. On the day of the party, go to Lidl. Meander your merry way to the alcohol aisle. Put two of everything, spirit-wise, into a giant trolley (as in, two bottles of whisky, two of vodka, two of gin, two of schnapps, two of brandy, etc.), plus a couple of boxes of wine for good measure.

Now go to the soft drinks aisle. Put one of everything fizzy (except water) into the trolley, not forgetting a few cases of their own-brand energy drink and two litres of their double-concentrated squash, in both orange and blackcurrant iterations. Now go and buy a brand new bin, one with a capacity of around 80 litres. Pour everything you bought at Lidl into the bin, and give it a mix with the end of a clean(ish) hockey stick. Chop up what

feels like most of an orange grove and put it in the bin (the new one full of punch, not your kitchen bin). Just before guests arrive, add three or four 2kg bags of ice cubes to the concoction.

Have fun with the DangerPunch™ and make sure no one – *no one* – puts baked beans in it before 9pm.

5 THINGS TO DO WITH A SIX-PACK OF SAUSAGES

I love sausages in all their forms, and frequently disgust my Scottish Man by buying packs of flaccid frankfurters, microwaving them and dipping them in barbecue sauce. I'm a complete slut for charcuterie, too, but in terms of versatility, I maintain that the most useful iteration of sausage is our British banger – so-called because they once contained so much water and rusk, as opposed to pork, they'd explode upon cooking. Here are five little ideas that show off the hidden talents of a pack of sausages; if you're veggie, 2,4 and possibly 5 will work with any plant-based bangers too.

1. FIVE-INGREDIENT SAUSAGE AND BEAN STEW GFO

If you have a pack of **sausages**, a big **onion**, some **mixed beans** and a tin of **tomatoes**, you can make this filling winter stew. What you do is squeeze the sausage meat out of the casing and into a hot frying pan containing 2 tablespoons of **oil**, breaking up the sausage with a wooden spoon to make it into smaller chunks. While that's frying, chop a huge onion into whatever size dice you want – it really doesn't matter here. When the sausage meat has got a bit of colour on it, remove it from the pan and put it in a bowl next to the hob, 'cos you'll want it in a tickle. Add your onion to the sausagey pan – it shouldn't need too much more oil as some fat will have come out of the meat – and fry until soft, adding in any **dried herbs** you're into. Return your sausage meat to the pan, followed by the tin of chopped tomatoes and the mixed beans (don't worry about draining them), then let that all simmer for 20 minutes or so, checking for seasoning periodically. Serve covered in **cheese** with a carbohydrate and possibly a vegetable. Makes roughly three portions.

2. TOAD-IN-THE-HOLE VO

I bloody love toad-in-the-hole. What an epic invention: sausages encased in a giant puffy Yorkshire pudding. You can make this one with veggie sausages if you want – it's exactly what Linda McCartney envisioned when she invented the concept.

What you do is make up a quantity of **pancake batter** according to the recipe on page 51 and let that rest while you cook off a pack of 6 **sausages** in a deep square roasting tray with some **veg oil** in the bottom. Pop them in the oven at 200°C for 20 minutes, then, remove the tray from the oven, shutting the door quickly as not to lose heat, and swiftly pour your batter into the tray. It should fit and spizzle at you, so be careful. Return it to the oven for another 20 minutes, or until it's golden and puffy – don't open the door in this time, or it'll sink. Serve with a thick tangle of onion gravy: make the **Franglais Onion Soup** on page 60, but only add a quarter of the water. Makes roughly three portions.

3. EASY SPAGHETTI AND MEATBALLS

This is one of the first recipes I ever learned to cook. It's roughly based on a Jamie Oliver number out of one of his Red Nose Day mini cookbooks from about 2007, but I've messed with it since.

Start by squeezing gobs of **sausage meat** from their casing and rolling in your palms to make balls. You want them around the size of a large marble. Fry these off in a pan with some **vegetable oil**, shuggling it around so they caramelise on all sides. Add a tin of **chopped tomatoes**, a splash of **red wine** and a good squeeze of concentrated **tomato purée**, plus a crumbled **beef stock cube**, some **dried oregano** and **basil**, and a splash of water from the kettle if it's looking dry. Let that simmer with the lid on for 10 minutes, then increase the heat to high and let it reduce it down for 5 minutes. Taste it for seasoning, then reduce the heat to low while you cook some spaghetti according to the packet instructions. The sauce makes three or four portions, roughly, but freezes well if you're only cooking for one or two. When you want to serve, stir the meatball sauce through the spaghetti (none of this sauce-on-top nonsense, please) and cover in an obscene quantity of **Parmesan**, plus some torn **fresh basil** leaves, if you have some.

4. BARBECUE SAUSAGES THE SMART WAY VGO GFO

Throughout the summer, my diet consists of 70 per cent barbecue food and 30 per cent pre-mixed tins of gin and tonic. This is brilliant, and I love it – except for one thing, and that thing is burned sausages. I find it disrespectful to burn any food, especially something as delicious as a sausage, so I've taken to using this nifty wee trick to cook up to 12 snarlers evenly at the same time. The technique comes from my dad, who for every six daft ideas has one really good one.

You'll need two skewers; metal is best, but wooden works fine if they've been soaked in water first. What you're doing is threading all the **sausages** onto the skewers, so that the skewers run through each sausage at either end, and the sausages are all lined up and attached. It's as if the skewers are a big fork lift and the sausages are small, porky pallets. Then you can simply lay them on the barbecue as one big sausage-bedframe. Just turn one long edge to flip all the sausages at once – and always cut one open to see if it's cooked through before serving. This also works for veggie sausages.

5. STICKY SAUSAGE, CHEESE AND APPLE BAP VO

My preferred way of cooking **sausages** at home involves slicing them down the middle and opening them out so that you get more surface area to go sticky when you fry them. It's quicker to cook them this way, too – you should try it. When one side is nicely caramelised, I flip them, then start grating a good wee chunk of strong **Cheddar cheese**. By the time that's grated, the other side of the sausages will have cooked through, so I sprinkle the cheese straight onto the butterflied sausages to melt it in the pan, then slice open a **crusty white roll** and smear it with **butter** and some **apple sauce** (you can fry apple slices in the same pan as the sausages if you don't have sauce). I then grab a handful of **rocket**, and make a bed to slide two cheesy sausages straight onto. A gob of **wholegrain mustard** goes really well here, too. OK, yes, fine: this is a recipe for a tarted-up sausage sandwich, but it's self-care. Don't @ me.

CHAPTER 5:
LOW AND SLOW, BRO

~~~~~~~~~~~~~~~~~~~~~~~~~~

Something beginning with 'pan' and ending in 'demic' happened not so long ago, and it shifted the way many of us worked. It hit me in my penultimate year of university, and I was genuinely the most miserable I've ever been. Looking for silver linings in a dark cloud of horror is a game to be played extremely tactfully, if at all, but one thing the pandemic meant is that I began to use an extra ingredient available to me that hadn't seen much love in my kitchen before: time.

Time adds a depth and roundness to many meals that MSG can only dream of. Cooking things for longer at a slower temperature is a well-known method around the world, especially in the south of the US, where low-and-slow barbecuing reigns supreme. It's my dream to go to a proper low-and-slow cook-up in Texas, where half a cow has been relaxing on top of smoky charcoal for a good 12 hours. The reason this slow cooking works so well on otherwise tough bits of meat is that the abundance of collagen (found in the connective tissue) breaks down at around 70°C, turning to gelatine and creating that dreamy melt-in-the-mouth texture. There are three recipes in this chapter that make use of this process: the Accidental Cheap Ragu (page 126), the Six-hour Pork Shoulder in Red Wine (page 131) and the Beef and Stout Stew-Pie (page 123).

However, slow cooking isn't just for tenderising tough bits of protein over a very long time. If you're working from home, it's a no-brainer to let the oven or the hob do the grunt work of slowly roasting vegetables, cooking stubborn legumes or simmering stock, all while you're sending emails or pretending to look interested on a Zoom call. As such, the recipes here aren't just about meat; they reflect the different ways you can use time when it comes to veggie and vegan food, too. They're all rather hands-off for the most part, but when it is time to get up from the old desk and stir something every couple of hours or so, it makes for a nice break.

The recipes in this chapter are designed to make around four portions, rather than my usual two. This is because the energy usage for slower cooking is higher, so it's worth making a few more meals at the same time to spread out the cost. These recipes all freeze really well; if you're into your batch cooking and have space in your freezer, feel free to double things. I am neither into batch cooking, nor have oodles of space in my freezer, so having just two extra portions for the days when I lack cooking gumption (hey, it happens) does me perfectly.

Lastly, you might be thinking that I've forgotten about slow cookers here. I would love to forget about slow cookers due to some awful childhood experiences involving tinned peaches, cornflour and chicken breasts (I'm not joking), so while I appreciate that they can be useful and use much less electricity than an oven, it'll take a *lot* of convincing to get me to go near one ever again.

BEEF AND STOUT STEW-PIE

Don't tell anyone I told you this, but stew is just pie without clothes on. Of course, the slow-cooked stew that makes up the filling of this particular pie is delicious, and absolutely fine to be eaten naked, but it just feels much more presentable when dressed in a golden suit of crisp, flaky puff pastry. And if you've not made a pie before, don't worry; this is a cheat's version where you don't even have to shape any pastry, let alone make the stuff.[1]

By the way, if you're skimming the ingredients list and thinking to yourself, *Hmmm, that 800g of stewing beef doesn't sound especially cheap, Miss Budget Cookbook Author*, then you'd be right.

The truth is, I've never made this pie with beef chunks bought at full price. They've always been yellow-stickered down, and I've always been lucky enough to find a few packets of them at a time lying there, forgotten in the supermarket chiller – but this has happened to me often enough that the recipe warrants being in the book. So, should you ever find yourself standing in front of a marked-down offer that would make a beef farmer turn inside out with hot, hot fury, then here's how to make the most out of it all.

Serves 3–4[2], takes 15 minutes (+15 minutes for pie) hands-on, 3.5–4 hours (+30 minutes for pie) to cook

YOU'LL NEED:

4 large carrots

2 white onions

beef dripping, lard or vegetable oil

800g diced stewing beef

3 teaspoons of plain flour

a few rosemary sprigs and a couple of bay leaves, if you have them

1.8 litres beef stock, made with 2 stock cubes

a 500ml bottle of stout or Guinness

2 teaspoons of wholegrain mustard or yeast extract (I use Marmite) (optional)

salt and freshly ground black pepper

To make it a pie:

500g puff pastry

an egg, for glazing (optional, but makes it pretty)

Chop your carrots into big, chunky 3cm lengths, and roughly chop your onions into large-ish pieces.

Get a big pot hot on the stove over a high heat and drizzle or spoon in a few tablespoons of either beef dripping, lard or vegetable oil. Tip in half your beef chunks, along with a big pinch of salt and a teaspoon of flour, and stir until there's some good colour on the beef, around 5-7 minutes. Take these browned chunks out of the pan and set aside on a plate, then repeat with the second batch of beef. Remove that batch from the pan too, then add a bit more fat and fry your onions in it, seasoning them with black pepper and a

---

[1] I've only ever made puff pastry once, when I was on a self-catering holiday in north-west Scotland. I was responsible for the food all week, and had planned to make this pie halfway through. However, I'm a wazzock, so forgot the puff pastry, and only realised when I got there. The nearest supermarket was two and a half hours away, so I spent an afternoon with a wine-bottle rolling pin and enough butter to kill a man, making my own. And while it worked perfectly well, and was extremely tasty, I learned from that experience that I will never, ever forget the puff pastry again.

[2] This is *meant* to serve 3-4 with a side of mash and peas, but whenever I make it, my pie-demolishing Scot can happily eat half of it before I've even had a chance to get the tatties cooked through.

pinch more salt, and scraping the bottom of the pan as you go. You want to get all that delicious brownness on the bottom of the pan from the beef (the technical term is *fond*) into the onions, as that's where the flavour really begins to build.

When your onions are really nice and soft, pop your beef chunks back into the pan, along with the rosemary sprig and the bay leaves, if you have them. Then, sprinkle over a final teaspoon of flour, stir it well, and pour in your beef stock and all but the last centimetre of stout – keep this for a bit later. Add the mustard, or even a teaspoon or two of yeast extract, if you like. Bring to a rapid boil, then pop on a lid at a jaunty angle so that some steam can still escape. Reduce the heat to low, and let your stew bubble grumpily for the next 3½–4 hours, stirring very occasionally. Fish the rosemary sprig out after the first hour, or it could make everything go slightly bitter.

When it's ready, you'll be looking for the stew's volume to have reduced by between a third and a half, and for the carrots to be completely softened. The sauce should have thickened significantly, so if you're in any doubt, bring it to the boil for another 10 minutes. Taste and season everything again here, then add the final dribble of stout to bring that flavour back to the forefront of everyone's minds. Remove the bay leaves.

You can now either freeze half of this and have the rest for dinner as a stew with mash, or make a pie with the whole lot.

TO MAKE A PIE:

To make a pie, preheat the oven to 200°C, and generously grease a 23cm springform or loose-bottomed cake tin.[3]

Roll out your pastry into a roughish circle, around 4–5mm thick – you don't want it too thin here, or it won't stand up on its own. Whatever shape you've ended up with should be really rather large – larger than the area of the cake tin by at least two-thirds. Now what you want to do is lift the pastry carefully into the cake tin, making sure the centre of the pastry sits in the middle of the tin, and the edges massively overhang the sides. Now lightly press the pastry into the bottom and the edges of the tin, making sure there are no gaps or holes forming. Carefully pour in your stew. It should come nearly to the top of the tin, but not quite. Next, roughly fold in the pastry edges on top of the stew, letting them sit in whatever way they want to. You could trim any excess pastry here, if you like, but I tend not to bother as my Scottish Man likes the slightly thicker, slightly stodgier bits you get when the pastry overlaps lots. It should look rough and ready and haphazard. Brush the entire thing with a beaten egg[4] if you want it to be shiny, then bake it in the oven for 30 minutes until everything is golden brown and puffy and looks amazing.

To serve, unclip the cake tin and remove the pie carefully, then pop it onto a serving plate. It should stand up by itself if you've rolled the pastry thickly enough and the stew was reduced properly, but if it collapses, then it'll be funny but still delicious. Enjoy with a side of mash and peas.

[3] You make my rockin' world go round.

[4] I always keep the rest of the beaten egg in the fridge (covered) and add it to scrambles or cakes, because I don't like throwing things away and it seems rude for the poor chicken's effort go to waste. It'll be fine for up to 5 days.

ACCIDENTAL CHEAP RAGU GF DF

I don't usually write recipes out of disgruntlement, but this one is an exception. It's in here because the oxymoronic concept of a 'quick Bolognese' needs to be bopped on the head with a big hammer, then buried somewhere so it can't escape to come back and haunt you with its complete lack of flavour. My annoyance will probably seem unreasonable until you, too, taste the difference between a pot of Bolognese or ragu that's been cooked in a hurry, versus one that's been left to simmer for *at least* two hours.

I discovered this method by accident, when I forgot about my Bolognese on the hob for four or so hours while I went to a talk about whether the communicative noises exchanged between macaque monkeys counted as language.[1] When I came back to my flat, I panicked upon seeing that the stove was still on, but I shouldn't have been worried. Reader, it was the meltiest, dreamiest, richest ragu I'd ever had. And I've not made it any other way since.

If you're working from home, I recommend that you start this at breakfast time (prep takes around 20 minutes), then leave it on the lowest heat for a few hours for a fabulously rich, filling lunch.

Serves 4, takes 30 minutes of hands-on work, and 2½–4 hours to cook, depending on how much you value **flavour**

YOU'LL NEED:

1 large carrot

2 large onions

1 giant celery stick, or 2 smaller ones[2]

olive oil

a tablespoon of double-concentrated tomato purée

450g beef mince that's over 15 per cent fat – I use the 25 per cent stuff, as it's the cheapest by far and adds lots of moisture and flavour

2 tins of tomatoes, either chopped or whole peeled plum

300ml red wine, or, if that's not possible, 300ml beef stock and 2 tablespoons of vinegar

salt and freshly ground black pepper

OPTIONAL EXTRAS:

a teaspoon of dried oregano

2–3 bay leaves

Start by chopping the carrots, onions and celery into the smallest dice you can muster. Heat up a couple of tablespoons of olive oil in a large saucepan over a medium heat and begin to fry this mixture, seasoning with a pinch of salt, some freshly ground black pepper and the oregano, if you're using it. Pop on the lid and leave everything to soften for a wee bit, then add your tomato purée and give it a good stir to stop it sticking.

Now, at this point, lots of recipes would suggest browning the beef off separately, but I've not noticed a huge difference between minced beef that's been subjected to a bit of browning and minced beef that hasn't, especially as it's all being cooked down with lots of wine and tomatoes for

---

[1] No, it doesn't. Do I regret my linguistics degree, you ask? Hmm. Tricky one. No comment.

[2] I've said it elsewhere, but if you won't use a whole pack of celery within a week or so, then it's best you don't bother buying it at all and just stick with onions and carrots to save on food waste.

ages. So, I just plonk the packet of beef in with the sofrito (that's the mix of vegetables you've just finely diced and fried), and break it up with a wooden spoon as it cooks. You may need to add a splash more olive oil, but do be aware that the beef, if you're using cheap stuff, will provide an awful lot of fat later on. Add a half teaspoon of salt here, too, to help everything along.[3]

When you're happy that the beef is cooked through, add your tins of tomatoes, breaking them up with the spoon if you need to. Let that all come up to temperature, then add your wine and some more seasoning. I will admit here that this is a very wine-heavy ragu, but that's the way I like it. You can use half-wine, half-stock if you'd prefer. Now, bring everything to a vigorous boil for 5 minutes, then reduce the heat to as low as it'll go. Taste for seasoning here, but remember that the ragu will reduce by around a quarter over the allotted time, so don't go too heavy on the salt. Add your bay leaves if you have them, then pop on the lid and leave for about 4 million years, or, as I said, *at least* 2 hours. The longer, the better, but check on the ragu every hour or so, and add a little boiling water from the kettle if it's looking at all dry.

What you're looking for when it's done is a rich sauce, where the beef has sort of melted in with the tomatoes and neither are distinct anymore. You should be able to taste the wine as if it were ambient lighting, bathing the whole thing in a warm, grown-up background glow; it should have lost all of its brightness. With any luck, you'll also get pools of orange fat on the surface. Terrible people might have a mind to skim that off or dab at it with a kitchen towel, but if you know anything, it's that this is where the flavour lives, so stir it all back in. It should taste rich, but have a resounding mid-level tang to it, thanks to the tomatoes.

This freezes and defrosts incredibly well, so I tend to stir around a third of it through some freshly cooked pappardelle and top it with some Parmigiano for lunch, then spoon the rest into a few individual Tupperwares to cool before freezing. Here are some other serving suggestions, though:

• •

Go beyond Bolognese and have this ragu stuffed into (cooked) giant pasta shells, then baked under a big layer of melty cheese.

Slop the ragu into a round cake tin, then top with very thin slices of potato before drizzling with a little olive oil and salt, and baking for 25 minutes at 200°C.

Add 2 squares of dark chocolate, a tablespoon of smoked paprika, some chilli flakes and some ground cumin before simmering for a take on chilli con carne. Stir in 2 tins of kidney beans 20 minutes before serving (don't add them sooner, or they'll turn to mush).

When cold, spread the ragu over some bread and then grill it with some cheese on top to make UnWelsh Rarebit.

Use as a topping for baked potatoes.

• •

---

[3] Other recipes also call for Worcestershire sauce, brown sauce, bacon lardons or even Maggi cubes, but because this ragu is cooked for so long, these glutamate-boosting ingredients aren't needed. Time does all the work of deepening the flavour for you. I won't be mad if you add a couple of tinned anchovies in with the beef, though – that's an Italian power move right there.

SICILIAN-STYLE AUBERGINE STEW (VG) (GF)

Whenever I ask my friends what they'd like to eat, they look blankly at me as if to say, 'We really don't have a sodding clue.' So I reel off a list of possible suggestions, which always includes a curry, a roast, a risotto, and the word 'caponata'. Inevitably, they ask me, 'What is this caponata you speak of, Freeborn?', and I reply with, 'It's a sour Sicilian stew made with lots of olive oil, aubergines, tomatoes and capers, lifted by a heavy hit of red wine vinegar in the final moments of cooking. People usually add pine nuts, but look, I'm not made of money, so toasted chopped almonds will have to do if you want me to cook this for you.' Then, their faces light up and they say, 'We would very much like to eat that, please and thank you.'

This recipe is closely based on caponata but with more flexibility with the ingredients. It freezes well, so if cooking for fewer than four people, you can save portions for when you need a hit of hearty instant deliciousness.

Serves 4 as a main or 6 as a side, takes 30 minutes of hands-on work and around 1 hour to cook, plus 2–4 hours optional vibe time resting on the hob

YOU'LL NEED:

a third of a mug of good olive oil

2 large or 3 smaller aubergines

4 shallots, if you can find them, or 2 medium white onions if you can't

2 garlic cloves (optional)

2 tins of chopped tomatoes or peeled plum tomatoes

a tablespoon of raisins (*exceedingly* optional, but very authentic)

2 tablespoons of double-concentrated tomato purée

a smallish glass or half a mug of red wine (about 150ml)

a good tablespoon of capers (if your palate hasn't yet reached maturity, you may leave these delicious morsels out)

2 tablespoons of pitted olives, or more if you like them (I'll use whatever's in the cupboard or fridge; it doesn't matter if they're green or black. Again, if you're not a culinary chad, you can leave these out)

4–5 tablespoons of EITHER (in order of preference) red wine vinegar, balsamic vinegar, white wine vinegar or malt vinegar[1]

salt and freshly ground black pepper

2 tablespoons of pine nuts, if the budget allows, or the same quantity of chopped almonds if it doesn't, to serve

a good handful of fresh basil, if you want, to serve

Method this way ⟶

---

[1] One of the funny things about Italian cuisine is how regimented peasant dishes such as caponata have become. A real nonna would have used whatever she had available back in the day. Regarding the different vinegars, though, each one will change the character of the dish slightly – balsamic will be sweetest, and white wine will be sourest – but what you're after is that top note of acidity, which comes with any sort of vinegar. Caponata is often preserved in jars, so I imagine the vinegar helped with the preservation process as well as making things completely delicious.

SICILIAN-STYLE AUBERGINE STEW
CONTINUED ⟵

Pour your olive oil into a large, deep saucepan – it should definitely cover the bottom and come up the sides a little. Place over a medium heat. As it warms up, roughly chop your aubergines into oblongs of around 2–3cm. Add them to the pan, along with some salt, and fry them, stirring often, until the oil has soaked in and there's a little bit of golden-brown colouring on the flesh – around 6–8 minutes. You may need to do this in batches to get some properly nice browning.

Just as the aubergines are colouring, remove them from the pan and set aside in a bowl – you'll want them again in just a minute. There should be a small amount of olive oil left in the pan. Finely chop and fry your shallots or onions with a pinch of salt in this oil, adding more if necessary. Cover until they're translucent and cooked through, around 10 minutes. Add the garlic halfway if you're using it. Then, return the aubergines to the pan and fry for a little longer. Next, add your tins of chopped tomatoes, breaking up any plum ones with a spoon as you go. Add a good pinch of salt now, and a grinding of black pepper, along with your raisins, if they're going in. Squeeze in the tomato purée and add the red wine, then stir and simmer for around 45 minutes–1 hour with a lid on.

Once that time is up, stretch and have a cup of tea, then take the chance to add the capers and olives, if using. Next, pour in your vinegar. It should smell really sour at this point, and have a good acidic top note when you taste it, but with a deep richness underneath from all that previous simmering.

Adjust for seasoning (does it need more acidity? Or perhaps salt? Or maybe it's too tangy for you and you need a splash of olive oil?[2]). When you're happy, let it simmer – uncovered – for around 10 minutes while you doom-scroll. You *can* serve it now, but it's much better if you switch off the heat and leave it on the hob to meld for a few hours, reheating when you want to serve it.

To serve, toast the almonds or pine nuts in a dry frying pan and scatter them over the pot, along with some torn fresh basil leaves.

Caponata is usually served as a side, but we've taken to having this dish as part of an Italian-themed main, served with lots of focaccia (see page 171), some antipasti, such as artichokes and salami, and a huge green salad.

[2] Don't mention this to the polizi, but you *could* add a cheeky tablespoon of pesto here. Shhhhhh.

SIX-HOUR PORK SHOULDER IN RED WINE GF

This is the only proper cut of meat in the book, because it's one of the most economical whole joints you can buy. Pork shoulder is incredibly tender and juicy, due to its high fat content. It can be roasted quickly and scored to produce crackling, which is great – don't get me wrong – but I generally prefer it cooked for hours and hours at a lower temperature, drowned in wine, to produce deeply flavoursome, melt-in-the-mouth pulled pork. One day, I want to try cooking this outside over glowing embers in a blackened cast-iron pot, but the opportunity has never presented itself (mainly because I still have to get round to buying a cast-iron pot).

This cooks slowly over five or so hours in a low oven. If you're concerned about energy usage, you can cook it overnight, when the energy tariff is lower. Give it eight hours at 100°C; put it on when you go to bed and wake up to the smell of boozy pork. Alternatively, you can fill the rest of the oven space with potatoes (reheat them in the microwave for an easy baked-potato lunch) or slow-cook the veg for the soup on page 135 while the pork goes about its business being stonkingly rich and delicious.

Serves 4 as part of a hearty main meal, takes 6 hours, hands-on time 10 minutes

YOU'LL NEED:

1.5–1.8kg boneless pork shoulder

2 teaspoons of dried sage

5 whole cloves (optional)

6 garlic cloves

3–4 medium red onions

500ml red wine (literally anything goes here; I use the cheap table-wine from Lidl)

salt and freshly ground black pepper

OPTIONAL EXTRAS:

Creamy Dreamy Mishmash (page 39), to serve

toast, to serve

red cabbage slaw or a green salad, to serve

Find an ovenproof pot with a tightly fitting lid that you know will be big enough to hold the pork shoulder, alongside a handful of onions. One of those posh cast-iron ones would be very helpful here.

Score the pork's skin in a criss-cross pattern, then rub the joint of meat with around a tablespoon of salt, a very good layer of black pepper and the dried sage, working these into all the nooks and crannies. Push in the whole cloves here and there, if you're using them. Peel the garlic cloves and push them under the skin of the pork, and into any natural crevices you can find within the muscle structure.

Peel and chop the onions into quarters, then lay them in the bottom of the pot. If they don't all fit, that's fine; the rest can sit around the pork later. Place the pork on top of the onions, fat-side up (the fat protects the meat from burning) and squodge any remaining onions around the pork. Now for the fun bit: glug the wine over the whole thing, pop on the lid and bop it in the oven, which you can now turn on at 140°C.

SIX-HOUR PORK SHOULDER IN RED WINE CONTINUED ←——

Cook the pork for up to 6 hours at this temperature. It's very forgiving, so will be done after just over 5 hours. Remember to baste it every hour or so; just do it whenever you need to get up from your desk. Basting, if you're unfamiliar with the concept, is when you pour the meat juices over the meat periodically to keep everything moist. You can do this with a big spoon. If it's looking in the least bit dry at any point, add some more wine or some stock to keep it all juicy. If you feel it's really getting dry too fast, you might have an oven that runs hot or a lid that doesn't fit tightly enough, so turn it down by 10°C.

When everything is meltingly tender and the onions are so gooey they longer even resemble onions, you can serve. If you want to, you can make a gravy with a little flour and the porky juices, but I think the cooking liquid makes an amazing sauce just as it is. I often break up the pork into the juices and let everyone just help themselves at the table, which keeps things very moist and warm. Serve with lots of creamy mash to soak up the juices, or some lovely toast, but also something acidic to cut through things a little. I like a very tangy red cabbage slaw (thinly sliced red cabbage, sesame oil, red wine vinegar, caraway seeds, pickled gherkins) or a giant green salad dressed with enough lemon juice to turn your face inside out.

ROASTED BUTTERNUT SQUASH, PEANUT BUTTER AND CHILLI SOUP

This soup comes together very quickly after the oven has done all the hard work for you. You don't even need to peel the squash or fry the onions. What you will need, however, is a handheld electric blender, a smoothie maker or a food processor, so do find yourself one of those before you go to the effort of roasting everything, only to swear loudly because you don't have one for the last step.[1] If you want any encouragement to go out and get one immediately, this soup is what it feels like to drink warm orange velvet. It's magically smooth and creamy, and is absolutely the perfect thing to eat with nice brown bread after a day of doing

something wholesome, like knitting your pet goldfish a jumper. If that's not a reason to buy a stick blender, I don't know what is.

As always, play around with quantities of peanut butter and chillies at the blending stage. I'm a big wimp, so only like a gentle, warming spice with a little zing on top, but feel free to go full-blown spice monster here if you're that way inclined.

Serves 4 as a main course, takes 20 minutes of hands-on work, 2.5 hours to cook

YOU'LL NEED:

1 enormous butternut squash, or 2 small ones (about 1.5kg unpeeled)

2 big white onions

olive oil

a teaspoon of chilli flakes

2 vegetable stock cubes

around a third of a jar of smooth peanut butter (about 80g/4–5 tablespoons)

a red mild chilli, or more if you'd like it to bite back, plus extra to serve

a tablespoon of apple cider vinegar, or juice of ½ lime

salt and freshly ground black pepper

fresh coriander, to serve (optional)

vegan coconut yogurt, to serve (optional)

Quarter your squashes lengthways and scoop out the seeds, reserving them to sprout and grow squash vines in inconvenient places around your flat. Peel and then chop the onions in half. Place the squash quarters on a baking tray, cut-sides up, along with the onion halves, also cut-side up, and drizzle everything generously with olive oil before scattering over the chilli flakes, salt and freshly ground black pepper. Pop this in an oven set to 140°C (no need to preheat, as it's going to be in there for a long time and it doesn't matter about it being hot to start with). Cook for around 2–2½ hours,[2] or until the onion is nicely golden and the squash is soft all the way through.

[1] One of the funniest kitchen moments I've ever witnessed was when my friend Eve (the same Eve from page 48) was making pickled eggs in a beetroot-infused vinegar. She hadn't read the recipe through properly, and the final step was something like: 'Leave for a month to mature.' We all came running to the kitchen when she yelled 'WHAT!' in the angriest tone I'd ever heard come out of her mouth, then collapsed laughing when we found out that she'd wanted to make it to eat for lunch that day.

[2] While the oven is on this low, you could make the pavlova on page 115, bung in the six-hour pork on page 131, or simply fill the remaining space with potatoes to bake at the same time.

ROASTED BUTTERNUT SQUASH, PEANUT BUTTER AND CHILLI SOUP CONTINUED ←———

The assembly of this soup takes little more than 10 minutes, and the veg will quite happily vibe in the oven, switched off, until you want to make it, so use that information as you see fit.

To make the soup, boil the kettle and make up 1 litre of vegetable stock if you prefer a thicker soup, or 1.5 litres if you like it thinner – adjust your stock-cube usage accordingly, as soup is very easy to over-salt. Using a spoon, scoop out the flesh of the squash from the skin, and put it in a big pan, along with the onions, peanut butter and hot stock. Place over a medium heat to keep everything toasty. Chop your chilli(es) finely and add to the pot. Give everything a good stir and let the peanut butter melt a bit before going at it with the stick blender, or transfer it to a food processor or smoothie maker for a good 5 minutes to make sure everything is beautifully smooth.

When it's all safely back in the pan (if it had to have a hiatus in a food processor), you can channel your inner Remy from *Ratatouille* for 5 minutes and make some adjustments. If you want it to be thinner, add more stock. If you want it to be thicker – well, that's a bit more challenging now you've added all your squash, but a tin of butter beans or cannellini beans blended in will fix that if you're really fussed about it. Now, give it a taste. Because you've been cautious with the salting, it could need a dash more. If you think it could do with more chilli (and bear in mind, you'll be eating a whole bowl of it, so be careful and have a few spoonfuls before deciding), chop up another half chilli and blend it in. What it probably will need, above all, though, is a tiny hit of acid, so micro-dose it with a tablespoon of vinegar or some lime juice, blend it, then taste again.

When you want to serve the soup, ladle it into bowls and top with a swirl of coconut yogurt, if it needs it, and some freshly chopped coriander, along with a few fine slices of red chilli.

YELLOW SPLIT PEA DAL (VG) (GF)

Dal is both the Hindi word for pulses, and the word for the dish made from them, and there are as many different ways to make dal as there are fish in the sea. This is the recipe I use. Naturally, I can claim diddly squat in terms of authenticity or authority on this one, but the principle of cooking the pulses first, then adding separately cooked (tempered) onions and spices is generally the way it's done. Also note that yellow split peas are different to chana dal in that they're less flavoursome, but more readily available where I live. You can, of course, use chana dal here but you may need to increase the cooking time if so.

I love making this in the dead of winter, just after Christmas when the old bank balance is looking low and I need something warming and filling to cheer me up. I also don't like leaving half-packets of things in the cupboards, because I'm prone to spilling them all over the floor, so this one makes use of a whole bag of yellow split peas. Feel free to halve the recipe below if you don't have the friends to feed or freezer space to fill.

Serves 6 as a hearty main, takes 20 minutes of hands-on work, 2–3 hours to cook

YOU'LL NEED:

500g yellow split peas

1.8 litres of water

a mouse-sized chunk of fresh ginger

3 large garlic cloves

2 large onions

a mild red chilli

4–5 tablespoons of vegetable oil (or ghee if you're not plant-based)

2 teaspoons of ground turmeric

2 teaspoons of ground cumin

a teaspoon of ground coriander

a tablespoon of garam masala

salt

rice and/or roti, to serve

OPTIONAL EXTRAS:

spinach

a block of coconut cream

Empty the yellow split peas into a large saucepan with the water, then place over a gentle heat. Chop half of the ginger into slices of about the same thickness as a pound coin, and do the same to one garlic clove before throwing them into the split peas, along with a teaspoon of salt, to help flavour everything. Leave this to bubble on the stove over a very low heat for around 2–3 hours.[1] Try to stir it every 45 minutes or so while this is happening, to stop any sticking. If it's looking at all dry, add a splash more water. Skim off any scum as you go. Start testing the peas for doneness at the 2 hour mark – everyone's peas, stoves and pots are different, so this will vary. What you're after is for the peas to be soft all the way through, and just losing their structure. Like many of the recipes in this chapter, you can leave this to cool down if you're not ready to finish things off yet.

[1] If you want to do a speedier version of this, you can soak the split peas overnight and put them on a rapid boil for around 40 minutes, but this is low and slow because I do it when working from home, and it's nice to let things take their time.

YELLOW SPLIT PEA DAL
CONTINUED ←——————

When you feel like doing the final stages, grate the remaining ginger and garlic on the large side of a box grater, then chop the onions into 1cm dice and finely chop the red chilli. Add these to a separate frying pan, along with the vegetable oil and spices. Cook this heady mixture slowly, with a lid on, until the onions are gloriously soft, which will take around 10–15 minutes.

When you want to serve, discard the big chunks of ginger and garlic before they assault someone's mouth, then stir those slippery onions into the split peas over a gentle heat. You can wilt some spinach in here, or make it extra creamy by melting in one of those blocks of coconut cream that always solidifies, so you have to peel the plastic off it like a room-temperature ice lolly.

Serve hot with roti, or rice. Or both.

5 THINGS TO DO WITH PUFF PASTRY

Ready-rolled puff pastry is more expensive than the frozen blocks you can buy, but I use both interchangeably, depending on my mood. I only bought a rolling pin recently, because it was a quid in a charity shop, but before that I would use a wine bottle, a full can of lager or, least effectively, a Sports Direct mug. You'll want to be using pastry that's rolled to a thickness of about 3mm: around the width of the tip of a USB stick, or, for the conventional among us, a little thicker than a pound coin.

1. THREE-INGREDIENT BRIE AND CRANBERRY TARTLETS (PERFECT FOR A CHRISTMAS PARTY) V

Roll out your **puff pastry** until it's USB-stick thick. Thoroughly grease a muffin tin and cut the pastry into squares roughly the size of a small coaster. Pop each square into a muffin hole and fill the nookity-bit of each one with a thumb-sized wodge of **brie** and a teaspoon of **cranberry sauce**. Fold the corners of the tarts in on themselves, then bake at 210°C for 15–20 minutes, or until Gordon Brown all over. Leave to cool for at least 5 minutes before tucking in, or you'll ruin the rest of the festive eating period with mouth burns. Guess how I know that?

2. BROWN SUGAR AND CINNAMON PINWHEEL VGO

Roll out your **puff pastry** to a £1-thick rectangle and spread it with softened **butter or vegan spread**. Now sprinkle over a generous layer of **brown sugar** – either demerara or soft light brown is perfect, but white will do, too, if that's all you have. Next, sprinkle over a very good dusting of **cinnamon**. Roll up the pastry from the shorter edge like a naughty carpet and wrap the resulting tube tightly in clingfilm. Chill in the fridge for 15 minutes or so, or longer if you're making these ahead. (By the way, nothing bad will happen if you don't refrigerate them, but they might unravel slightly more when cooked.) When you're ready to bake them, preheat the oven to 210°C and slice the roll into 1cm thick slices (you get the wonky first and last slices straight out of the oven; chef's treat). Arrange on greaseproof paper on a flat baking tray and bake for 10–12 minutes, keeping a watchful eye, as these tend to burn very quickly. You can mix a little **icing sugar** and some water to make a glaze to drizzle over if you want to be extra, but these are cracking wee treats just as they are.

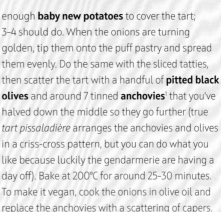

3. THE EASIEST, HOTTEST JAM PUFFS IN THE WORLD (VGO)

Roll out your **puff pastry** to 1€ thick (take that, Nigel Farage) and stamp out an even number of circles using a big wine glass – or, if you have such a thing, a round cookie cutter of a similar circumference. Divide the circles into two groups and mentally designate them as lids and bases. Blob a teaspoon of your **favourite jam** in the middle of the bases, then run a damp finger around the perimeter of the jam blob before popping on a lid. Don't overfill them, or they'll explode. That's a threat.

Pinch together the lid and base at the edges, first using your fingers and then using a fork so that it sticks properly and looks pretty. You can glaze them with a beaten **egg** here if you want them to look presentable. Egg or no egg, poke a four-pronged hole in the top of each tart to allow steam to escape and bake for around 15 minutes at 190°C. Hot jam is essentially sticky fruity lava, so make sure you let these cool for at least 10 minutes before going at them. They're lovely with a dob of **clotted cream** if you want to serve them for pudding, but do equally well as a portable snack.

4. FANCY FRENCH TART (VGO)

This is very fancy but surprisingly cheap and delicious, using the chad-like flavours of anchovies, onions and black olives. It's based on *tart pissaladière* from Nice, but I always introduce some Scottish carb-on-carb action by adding a layer of very thinly sliced new potatoes. Finely slice three small **white onions** into half-moons, then fry them in **butter** while you unravel or roll some **puff pastry** onto a lined baking sheet. Thinly slice

enough **baby new potatoes** to cover the tart; 3–4 should do. When the onions are turning golden, tip them onto the puff pastry and spread them evenly. Do the same with the sliced tatties, then scatter the tart with a handful of **pitted black olives** and around 7 tinned **anchovies**[1] that you've halved down the middle so they go further (true *tart pissaladière* arranges the anchovies and olives in a criss-cross pattern, but you can do what you like because luckily the gendarmerie are having a day off). Bake at 200°C for around 25–30 minutes. To make it vegan, cook the onions in olive oil and replace the anchovies with a scattering of capers.

5. MARMALADE CHOCOLATE CRACKER (VGO)

This requires very little mental effort and is always a winner of a pud – even if it's not Christmas. It's also vegan, if you're using cheap puff pastry.

Preheat the oven to 200°C. Roll out a roughly A4-sized rectangle of **puff pastry** and orientate it to portrait rather than landscape. Spread the pastry with a layer of **marmalade**,[2] leaving an inch-thick marmalade-free margin at the edges, then put a 100g bar of **dark chocolate** right in the middle. Fold over the long edges of the pastry and make an overlapping seam down the middle of the chocolate bar. Make sure this overlaps by at least an inch, so everything is contained and you don't get leaky chocolate. Now pinch the pastry together at the top and bottom of the chocolate bar, so it forms a Christmas-cracker shape. Turn the cracker over, seam-side down, and make three light slashes in the middle with a knife. Brush with **beaten egg** and sprinkle with **sugar** before baking for 15–20 minutes, or until puffy and golden. Dust with **icing sugar** and serve in thick slices with **vanilla ice cream**.

---

[1] Use the rest of the open tin of anchovies in Mediterranean Chicken Stew with Olives But Not Sun Cream (page 71) or Accidental Cheap Ragu (page 126), or use them to add non-vegan depth to Mushroom, Ale and Lentil Pie on (page 53).

[2] Use the rest of the marmalade in the Hot Jam Puffs above, or to glaze the sausages in my Sausage, Squatternut Bosch and Red Onion Traybake (page 56). You could even mix it with chilli and smoked paprika, microwave it for 20 seconds and brush it all over the Spatchcocked Chicken in the Dead of Night (page 43). Or put it in a cheese toastie instead of chutney.

CHAPTER 6:
HELLO, SWEETIE

~~~~~~

In my world, a day without something to violently elevate my blood glucose before bed is a day wasted. I think we neglect proper dessert here in the UK, shunning it in favour of a sweet treat with a coffee, or a chocolate bar snaffled at your desk mid-morning, but I maintain that eating a good pudding is one of the most pleasurable things on the planet, besides sticking an index finger straight into a new tub of body butter.

Luckily, desserts are a very easy thing to do properly. You just have to think about four things: sweetness and punch, and softness and crunch. By 'sweetness and punch', I mean making sure something has the right balance of bitterness and acidity for the amount of sugar used. A perfect demonstration of this is the fact that sugar dissolved in water is cloyingly sweet and unpleasant, but when you add lemon juice and put it in a fancy bottle with cursive writing all over it, suddenly it's remarkably refreshing and moreish. Good examples of elements in desserts that add bitterness or acidity are very dark chocolate, coffee, some alcohols, tart fruit compotes or jam, black treacle, burnt caramel and, of course, citric juices.

By 'softness and crunch', I mean making sure everything's not just the same texture throughout. It doesn't have to be crunchy, per se – I mean, I'd be worried if my tiramisu was crunchy – but it's nice to have contrasting textures in a dessert. Many desserts (baklava aside) are inherently soft. You can add crunch with broken biscuits or chopped toasted nuts, and, of course, a buttery biscuit base or a crumbly, crisp shortcrust does the same thing.

The recipes in this chapter are all takes on classics really, starting with a lemon and raspberry Eton Mess, and ending on a deluxe affogato. There is also a hot chocolate recipe halfway through, which is rich and creamy enough to 100 per cent count as dessert if you make it the way I do, using lashings of double cream, nutmeg and orange zest. The added advantage to many of these recipes is that they can also serve as breakfast the next day, because anything's healthy if you add a big dollop of Greek yogurt and some oats. Probably.

And finally, if sweet things of any description set your teeth on edge, you can skip this chapter and go suck on an anchovy. I will forgive you, as long as you don't say something silly like 'oh, I'll have a cheeseboard for my pudding'. Yes, cheeseboards are delicious, but no, they are not pudding. Thank you for tedding to my come talk.

A quick note for the Americans and Europeans reading this: pudding is dessert. Not that grim custardy stuff you get in a packet and mix with milk. If we were still in the EU, I might be more lenient with my terminology, but we're not, for reasons I will never be able to fathom. The only advantage to Brexit, as I see it, is that we can still call dessert 'pudding' without anyone kicking up a fuss. Got it?

BASTARD RASPBERRY, LEMON AND PISTACHIO ETON MESS (V) (GF) (DFO)

I grew up in Cornwall, and my first ever relationship was with a lovely bloke called Pete. (We're still good pals today. He's an architect now. And a vegetarian.) Pete's mum, Tanya, who is an amazing cook, introduced me to this dessert when I was 16. The original recipe is called Eastern Mess and is from Sabrina Ghayour's book *Persiana*; it uses rosewater and basil alongside the raspberries, and is genuinely stunning.

Bastardising recipes, however, is one of my favourite things to do. I like to add lemon zest to the cream, then swirl lemon curd and raspberry coulis through it, along with the fresh raspberries, and I omit the rosewater and basil. So it's really not the same at all, but there we go. You now know where it has come from.

This can be assembled in 15 or so minutes, requires no further chilling, and you can use store-bought meringues (but don't tell Pete's mum I said that).

I make no apology for having two raspberry-based recipes in this chapter, because they're my favourite fruit. However, because this one calls for fresh raspberries as well as frozen (you can make it all with fresh if your budget allows, but fresh razzers are *expensive*), you're best making it in summer when raspberries are cheaper and more delicious. That said, you can replace the fresh raspberries with the same amount of chopped strawberries if you want, which are more reliable year-round.

I'm sure you could get creative with a pomegranate and clementine one at Christmas, or go for blackcurrant in the autumn, if you can get hold of them. Probably wouldn't have a springtime asparagus and lamb one, though – might be a bit odd with ripples of mint sauce running through it.

Serves 6, takes 20 minutes

YOU'LL NEED:

a bag of frozen raspberries (about 300g)

a small lemon, zested and juiced

a tablespoon or two of icing sugar

2 tablespoons (40g) of shelled roasted pistachios, unsalted

600ml double cream (Oatly now do a whippable plant-based cream, by the way, if you still want to make this but can't have dairy)

5 individual meringue nests

a punnet of fresh raspberries or strawberries (about 200g)

½ jar of lemon curd (200g or so)

OPTIONAL EXTRAS:

mint or basil leaves, to decorate

To start, defrost the frozen raspberries overnight in the fridge, or use the low-power option on the microwave. You can even quickly run them under a warm tap in a colander. Once defrosted, mash to a pulp with half the lemon juice and a little icing sugar, to taste, to make a coulis. Roughly chop the pistachios.

Whip the cream until it's floppy, adding the lemon zest halfway. I don't actually own an electric hand whisk, so I whip the cream with a large balloon whisk and some overdeveloped triceps. Whatever you do, don't overwhip it at this stage, as stirring stuff into it later finishes off the job. You're looking for ribbons here rather than peaks.

BASTARD RASPBERRY, LEMON AND PISTACHIO ETON MESS CONTINUED ⟵

Crush the meringues into bite-sized pieces and fold them through the cream, along with the punnet of fresh raspberries (reserve a few for garnish), a few dabs of the curd and coulis, and half of the pistachios. If you're serving it to people who really couldn't give a toss what it looks like, you can fold in the rest of the raspberries in here, and ripple through rivers of the curd and coulis softly in the same bowl. Serve with the rest of the lemon curd in the jar and the remaining pistachios for sprinkling, and let people help themselves.

If you're looking to impress, however, serving it in a large glass bowl is the way to go. Spaff some of your raspberry coulis and dollops of lemon curd around the bottom and sides of the bowl, then slide a quarter of the cream-and-meringue mixture on top. Dollop over some more raspberry purée and wee gobs of the curd, before layering up the rest of the mix in the same repeated manner. Top with the remaining pistachios, raspberries and some extra lemon zest.

Mint leaves or Sabrina's basil leaves really set off the red of the raspberry beautifully as a garnish, but that's entirely optional, as this is one of the more expensive recipes in this book as it is.

It's best to serve this right after you've made it, as the meringue goes soggy after a while, and the cream has a tendency to curdle when it's pressed up against all those acidic raspberries for longer than an hour or so.

BAKED PLUMS IN RED WINE (V) (VGO) (GF)

This is an absolutely gold-standard dessert. It's rich, grown-up, and ludicrously easy to prepare and bake. I think serving it with an unsweetened dairy, such as mascarpone or double cream, is the best way to complement the plums, but if you're a diehard ice-cream fan, go for it. You can use any bottle of cheap wine you like, because you're going to augment it with cinnamon and honey, and cook off all the alcohol anyway. As an aside, I have always got around the whole 'only cook with what you'd drink' mantra by being happy to drink literally anything. I even mull Buckfast at Christmas. Fear me.

Anyway, this dish is easily veganised if you use brown sugar rather than honey, and if you make sure your wine is vegan-friendly. There's a wide array of plant-based cream or ice-cream alternatives with which to serve it, too.

I think it's lovely with flaked, toasted almonds sprinkled over the top, but if you're pushed for time or can't be bothered with that, I won't mind too much.

Serves 4, takes 25 minutes

YOU WILL NEED:

a 450g punnet of red plums

300ml cheap red wine

5 heaped tablespoons (75g) of brown sugar, or equivalent in honey if you're not vegan-ing

½ teaspoon of ground cinnamon

a tub of cream, ricotta, mascarpone or vegan equivalent to pass around the table, to serve

OPTIONAL EXTRAS:

a pinch of ground cloves

60g toasted flaked almonds, to serve

Preheat the oven to 180°C. Split the plums in half and remove the stones. Lay them face up in a rectangular ceramic baking dish, so that they're nestled together but not too squished. Pour the wine over and around the plums, then scatter them with the sugar or drizzle with honey. Sprinkle with the cinnamon and ground cloves, if you have them, and bake for 25–35 minutes, or until the wine has gone syrupy, and the plums are just on the verge of not holding their shape anymore, and have nice caramelised bits around their edges.

When they're done, sprinkle with the toasted flaked almonds (tip a whole bunch into a dry frying pan and let them colour for 3–4 minutes, stirring), then bring the hot dish to the middle of the table with a metal serving spoon to let guests dish out their own servings and top with whatever dairy or non-dairy alternatives they fancy. If you've found that your plums haven't caramelised the way you wanted them to in the oven, sprinkle them with more sugar and shove them under a hot grill for 5 minutes before serving.

BAKED PLUMS IN RED WINE
CONTINUED ⟵

This dish also works with white wine and apricots; the below acrostic poem serves two:

~~~~~~~~~~~~~~~~~~~~~

Arrange halved, stoned apricots in a small baking dish

Pour over about 250ml of white wine

Runny honey should be squeezed over next

I like to add a sprinkle of demerara sugar, too

Cinnamon also and obligatory nutmeg

Oven temp is as above – bake for 20–30 minutes

The apricots should be soft and caramelised slightly, with the wine syrup bubbling away

Serve with cream or ice cream

~~~~~~~~~~~~~~~~~~~~~

Either of these recipes is utterly gorgeous in the morning spooned over thick Greek yogurt and topped with granola. Don't worry about mixing your mornings with wine-flavoured things – it works. I promise. Hic.

JAMMY FROZEN RASPBERRY CRUMBLE ⓥ ⓥⒼⓄ

To enjoy the best raspberries in the world, you have to wait until summer, teleport to the east coast of Scotland and go bonkers at a pick-your-own.

The obvious next-best option is to buy fresh raspberries at the supermarket, but that's often just a disappointing way to bankrupt yourself. But don't lose hope, dear reader, for there is a solution to all these berry-based woes. Yes, for far less than the price of fresh, you can purchase a big sack of raspberries, picked and frozen at their best, just ready for you to ping at unsuspecting flatmates. Or to put into this tangy raspberry crumble.

This crumble probably could serve four if you wanted it to. But it could also serve just you for pudding if you've only had olives for tea, and then just you for breakfast again. It's spaffingly good with vanilla ice cream, or extra-thick double cream – and the cream off the top of the coconut milk tin works equally well for plant-based pals: substitute vegan block instead of butter in the topping to make the whole thing animal-free.

Serves 4 (or just you), takes 30 minutes

YOU'LL NEED:

½ bag of frozen raspberries (around 250–300g)

75g butter, or something that might, probably, perhaps resemble butter if you squint

150g plain flour

6 or so tablespoons of caster sugar, to taste

OPTIONAL EXTRAS:

a handful of any chopped nuts/seeds you like – pecans work well

a pinch of ground cinnamon or nutmeg

a scattering of oats, if you're going to pretend it's healthier than it is

Tip your frozen raspberries into an 18–20cm cake tin, or a small baking dish. They should be 2–3 layers deep and clank pleasingly against the metal as you pour them in.

Preheat the oven to 180°C. Put the cake tin full of raspberries in the oven while it's warming up to defrost them without the splattering aggression of the microwave.

While your oven is heating up, make the crumble topping. If you have a blender or smoothie maker, weigh the butter and flour into it. Blend it on a pulse setting, if it has one, or in short bursts if it doesn't and you're using one of those tall smoothie-maker things. Shake the blender loads while you're doing it, as you don't want to overwork the mix. You're looking for a sandy texture, which most cookbooks describe as fine breadcrumbs, but I prefer to call 'butter graupel' as per my avalanche training. If you don't have the luxury of a blender, rub the butter into the flour using your fingertips and pretend you are Mrs Tiggy-Winkle from the Beatrix Potter stories.

Transfer this mixture into a bowl and add as much sugar as you see fit – I use around 4 heaped tablespoons (quarter of a coffee mug). Stir in any nuts, seeds, cinnamon, etc. you want to here, but if it's dessert rather than breakfast, don't worry about them. Add the oats, too, if you like.

Remove the warmed raspberries from the preheated oven and sprinkle over as much sugar as you feel necessary. I'm a tart girl myself, so don't need much sweetening up before I'm absolutely ready to go. I use about 1½ tablespoons, but you can always use more.

Now tip your crumble mix over the top of the raspberries and lightly press it down with your fingers so you get it all in.

Bake the crumble for 20 minutes, or until it's turned a deep Gordon Brown.

Once it's nicely coloured and the raspberries are making their bubbly debut around the edges, it's done. Let it cool for a wee bit, and then serve it either by itself or with whatever you like best with crumble.

To create the illusion of a healthy breakfast, I drizzle this with peanut butter and have it with yogurt, which I cannot recommend highly enough. It's also fabulous with lightly whipped whisky-spiked cream, as an impressive nod towards cranachan, the Scottish dessert served at a stonking number of twee tartan hotels just off the A9.

DELUXE AFFOGATO ⓥ

Affogato is Italian for 'drowned', because essentially you're suffocating a ball of vanilla ice cream with a shot of hot, strong espresso. That's it. So simple. And yet, the world is divided into the people who remember to make affogato, and the people who affogot that the matrimonial combination of strong coffee and sweet ice cream is the perfect end to a rich dinner. This is your reminder.

Below is my puddingy version of an affogato, complete with crushed amaretti biscuits, dark chocolate shavings and a splash of booze, should the mood take you. And, if you can get your hands on a jar of those gorgeous sour cherries in syrup that they sometimes have in the middle of Lidl, drop a couple in at the bottom and further culturally appropriate a simple and elegant dessert in the name of fun.

Vanilla is certainly the superior flavour of ice cream to use, but I'd imagine chocolate might also be acceptable as a sort of mocha version. Rum and raisin, caramel and honeycomb are not exactly traditional, but they will also work with the coffee. Avoid fruit-based ice creams, and don't even think about using mint choc chip, you heathen. Pouring Nescafé over a slice of Wall's Viennetta is not the goal here, and an Italian will cry – aggressively – if you do so.

Serves as many as you like, takes 10 minutes

YOU'LL NEED:

a scoop of ice cream for each person, preferably a nice vanilla with seeds in

2 amaretti biscuits each – failing that, digestives, shortbread or Hobnobs will suffice

a few sour cherries in syrup each, if you have them (don't use the ones from a tin – they're too sweet)

a square each of 70–80 per cent dark chocolate, grated or finely chopped with a knife

perhaps a splash of rum or amaretto, if you're feeling spunky

a shot of fresh espresso each, or 40ml very strong cafetiere coffee if you've no way to obtain proper espresso (use decaf if you're off to bed straight after)

Take the ice cream out of the freezer to soften as you start to make the coffee. Crush the biscuits however you like, but I find it's nice to have a range of crumb size for different textures. I crush mine in a sandwich bag, using a wine bottle. You could use a rolling pin, or a spare mannequin leg.

Affogato should be served individually in small glasses, tea cups or little ramekins. Choose your preferred receptacle, then, if you're using them, plop a couple of cherries in the bottom of each one with a teaspoon of the syrup. Scatter a tablespoon of crushed biscuit in the bottom of each, then scoop a ball of vanilla ice cream into each glass/cup/dish and sprinkle over the dark chocolate, which will melt quickly once the espresso hits it.

To serve, if you're using the booze, pour a splash over each ice-cream ball. Then, pour over the espresso shots and immediately top with the remaining crushed biscuits. Eat straight away.

To adjust this for sweet-toothed plebians, use milk chocolate, or sweeten the coffee before pouring over the ice cream – but I like it in all its slightly bitter glory. *Molto bene.*

CREAMY DREAMY HOT CHOCOLATE (V) (GF)

One of my favourite books in the world is Roald Dahl's *Charlie and the Chocolate Factory*, mostly because I like to think of myself as the 21st century, female equivalent of Willy Wonka (albeit without the goatee and with slightly more awareness of modern laws in child safeguarding). Anyway, early on in the book, there's a scene where Mr Wonka gives Charlie and his Grandpa Joe a cup of hot chocolate from the chocolate river, and it warms them up from the inside out with its thick, lovely creaminess. This recipe is about as close as I can get to this picture of fictional bliss – it's gloriously rich, but not too cloyingly sweet. Distressingly, however, there isn't a way of mixing this amount of hot chocolate by waterfall without diluting it homoeopathically – instead, I've gone for electricity, popping everything in the nearest blender to give it its characteristic velvety texture.

In the spirit of Mr Wonka, I tinker with this recipe each time I make it. Mint extract, vanilla, chilli powder, honey, grapefruit zest and the obligatory nutmeg and cinnamon have all found their way into this recipe at some point or another, but you should, of course, delve into the world of your imagination to see what you can come up with.

This recipe uses real dark chocolate, too, rather than any sort of powder, which I've always found far too sweet. You also get the added advantage of a very frothy top, as the proteins in the milk heat up and reform, much in the same way as foamy cappuccino milk made by a barista. If you don't have a blender or a smoothie maker, you can use a stick blender – or a balloon whisk and a dollop of elbow grease.

Serves 1, takes 5–10 minutes

YOU'LL NEED:

around 300ml milk (choose which type you like best – I use full-fat gold-top Jersey cream milk, because life is short and miserable and it is delicious)

2 large squares (40–50g) of 50–70 per cent dark chocolate – any higher, and it's too bitter

the tiniest pinch of salt

OPTIONAL EXTRAS:

a little splash of vanilla extract

a tiny pinch of ground cinnamon or nutmeg, or orange zest

cream, to serve (I'd happily mainline a tub of double cream on any given day, so this is a permanent fixture for me)

marshmallows, to serve

chocolate sprinkles, to serve

BLENDER METHOD

Grab your favourite mug. Give them a friendly kiss on the cheek and then tell them you're going to make them the best hot chocolate they've ever tasted. Find another mug and fill it with milk. If they complain, you have misidentified the type of mug I'm talking about, which is very silly of you.

Put the mug of milk in the microwave and zap it on high power for 2 minutes, or until the milk is piping hot (you can do this in a pan on the stove, too). Break up the chocolate chunks and drop them into the blender. If you're using a Nutribullet-style blender of the sort normal people would defile with fruit and protein powder, then drop them into the bottom of the flask bit and laugh at everyone else who uses this tool for smoothies rather than hot chocolate.

Pour the very hot milk on top of the chocolate pieces and add a tiny few granules of salt. Add any extracts, orange zest, cinnamon or nutmeg that tickle your fancy.

If you're using a sporty blender, screw the lid on and shake it about a bit. If you've got a jug blender, don't do this, or bad things will happen. This step is just to stop the chocolate melting to the top of the blender and not coming back down the sides again to be homogenised, if you see what I mean.

Blend everything on full power for at least a minute. The milk will expand and create so much wonderful froth that you might actually struggle to fit it all back into the same mug. No worries though, because you can chug the remainder straight from the blender like a gym bro, but one who's having much more fun.

STICK BLENDER OR BALLOON WHISK METHOD

Measure out 300ml milk into a microwavable jug. The reason you're doing it in a jug rather than a mug here is because you need room to mix everything properly later without making a giant mess. You can also do this in a big saucepan on the stove.

Microwave the milk on high power for 2 minutes, or bring it to a simmer, while you finely grate or chop your chocolate. When the milk is done, add any extracts/spices/zest, followed by the chocolate, and either blend with the stick blender, or whisk with the balloon whisk until everything is frothy and rich.

Whichever method you use, pour the hot chocolate into your favourite mug, and serve with softly whipped cream, chocolate sprinkles or some marshmallows if you're really chasing that insulin spike.

CHAPTER 7:
BAKED AF, DUDE

~~~~~~~~~~~~~~~~~~~~~~~~~~~~~~~~~~

Let me go all food-blogger on you for a minute.

When I was six years old, my mother bought me a pink, fairy-themed baking book from the Scholastic Book Fair. Having read the entire book that evening, I concocted a secret plan: I was going to wake up very early the next morning, and bake the pink-iced fairy cakes before school – all by myself.

When Mum came down to the kitchen at half-six the next morning, she was greeted by the sight of her tiny daughter transferring golden-brown cakes on to a cooling rack, proud as punch that the recipe had worked – no adult required. Never mind the streaks of cake mix on the walls. Never mind that I'd neglected to use a cupcake tin, so everything had spread out rather drastically in the cases on the baking tray. Never mind the sink full of bits of batter floating in the water. None of this mattered to me, because I'd done it all by myself, and had something decent to show for it.

In what I now realise was a great act of self-control, Mum quietly made herself a cup of tea and watched me drizzle luridly pink icing all over the cupcakes and the kitchen counter, before allowing me to take *two* whole fairy cakes to school in my lunchbox. She was very polite and encouraging about it all, but did request that, in the future, could I please do any baking *after* school, rather than just before it.

In the years since then, I've baked constantly. It's pure relaxation for me, with the added advantage of a box of homemade treats being a thoughtful gift, or simply a nice thing for others to come home to. You name it, I'll bake it. Pies, cakes, pastries, traybakes, tarts, bread; I love the entire process, from planning to scranning, and I really want to encourage others to enjoy it too.

The recipes in this chapter are just a tiny snapshot of the baking that I do, but they're chosen because, like a sweet-toothed moth on a light bulb made of sugar, I come back to them again and again. Even if you're a novice baker, you'll be able to make these recipes without rage-quitting halfway through, covered in flour and contempt. The only thing I ask of you is not to deviate too much from the quantities (or rather, ratios) given here. You can play around with all of the other food in the book without too much in the way of consequence, but baking is more of a science, so accuracy matters – and I wouldn't be mentioning it if I didn't think it was important. With that in mind, this is the only chapter where kitchen scales are borderline essential, but you don't need much else besides a small collection of different-sized tins, most of which can be borrowed or found for a few quid at the charity shop.

JANUARY MINCEMEAT MINCE PIES Ⓥ

Lots of people claim not to like mince pies, and for good reason – they've probably only had the mass-produced ones whose filling is too sweet, and whose pastry is claggier than eating a sheet of wet plasterboard. But homemade mince pies are a completely different, more buttery, ball game. If you've not made them yourself before, you should definitely have a go at least once. I make the majority of my mince pies in January, partially as a protest against that horrendous stream of 'New Year, New Me' diet culture, but mostly because jars of mincemeat go for less than 10p by Burns Night. All you need to do is make a batch of this beautifully short and buttery orange-spiked pastry to complement that bargain supermarket scoop.

Makes roughly 12, takes 1.5 hours

YOU'LL NEED:

125g chilled butter (if you're using unsalted, add a pinch of salt alongside the sugar, but salted butter will be just fine here), plus extra for greasing

200g plain flour

75g ground almonds

40g caster sugar, plus extra for sprinkling

2 teaspoons of freshly grated orange zest from a large orange

a large egg, beaten

a jar of mincemeat (around 300g)

a tablespoon of milk

Make sure your butter is completely fridge-cold before you start. Cut it into 1cm cubes, then place in a large bowl containing the flour and ground almonds, and use your fingertips to rub it all together until you have something that might possibly look a little like breadcrumbs. This will take about 7–8 minutes.

When that's done, mix in your caster sugar and orange zest. Now pour in the egg, and, using a table knife,[1] mix it gently to form a clumpy dough.

You may need to add a teaspoon of ice-cold water if your egg hasn't brought everything together properly, but go cautiously on the liquid here. Tip this rough mixture out onto a work surface and squeeze together lightly with your hands to form a more coherent, consistent dough, before wrapping it tightly in clingfilm and leaving it in the fridge for about half an hour to rest. That bit's important, by the way, so don't skip it, tempting though it is.

Preheat the oven to 200°C. Grease a 12-hole cupcake tin to within an inch of its life, or you won't be able to get the bastard things out, and that'd be terrible.

Roll out your dough until it's about the thickness of a £1 coin, then, using either a large wine glass or a proper cookie cutter, cut out discs of pastry around 9–11cm across, depending on the diameter and depth of your tin's little holes. Place them in the holes gently, then spoon in a couple of teaspoons of the mincemeat filling, making sure not to heap it in, or they'll burst and glue themselves onto the pan with hot, sticky, mincemeat-flavoured adhesive.

Gather the rest of the pastry scraps and re-roll them to the same thickness as before. Cut out lids using a different wine glass with a smaller

---

[1] This is to stop the heat from your hands melting the butter, and to bring it all gently together.

diameter, or use a jam-jar lid as a template if
you don't have either a smaller wine glass or an
appropriately sized cookie cutter. Top the pies
with the lids, then dip a little bit of kitchen roll in
some milk and brush it over (works just as well as
a pastry brush), then sprinkle with a touch more
caster sugar.

And don't worry if you have some mincemeat
or pastry left over; either use the tin again for
a second batch straight away, or do little handheld
mincemeat rounds without the need for a tin at
all – just enclose a heaped teaspoon of mincemeat
between two 9cm discs of pastry and bake it
on greaseproof paper on the shelf below the
'proper' pies.

Bake the pies for 20–25 minutes, or until a deep
Gordon Brown. Run a knife around the edges of
the pies as soon as they come out of the oven, to
avoid any mincemeat-adhesive situations, but then
leave them to cool in the tin for about 15 minutes,
as the pastry needs a little bit of time to regain
some structural integrity. Serve warm, with clotted
cream or brandy butter.

(Also, as an aside, I crumble a few of these mince
pies into a batch of cinnamon-infused vanilla ice
cream throughout December and January each
year. It sort of makes my daft impulse purchase
ice-cream maker worth the cupboard space.)

PLAIN JANE FRUITCAKE (V) (DFO)

Fruitcake, as well as being a gender-neutral term of affectionate derision, is one of those cakes left by the wayside a little. It's not as popular as its energetic lemon-drizzle cousin, nor is it as sweet as a carrot cake, or as family-friendly as an enormous chocolate cake covered in mascarpone icing (page 166). In the cake world, it could be mistaken for a bit of a plain Jane. But fruitcake has one amazing trick up its raisin: it's excellently, wonderfully, robustly portable.

Yep, you can wrap a dense brick of fruitcake in clingfilm or foil, and fling it into outer space with a fission-powered trebuchet. It'll be absolutely fine.[1]

In fact, if it's stayed up there, orbiting the Earth for a week or so, it'll be all the better for it. A second brownie point to fruitcake, then, is won by its nearly indefinite shelf-life. Of course, it tastes great on the day it's made, but like teenagers and good whisky, it could really do with being left alone to mature for a bit before you see it again. That said, a slice of warm fruitcake covered in butter, alongside a cup of tea, really does bits on a rainy afternoon. Save the rest for a few days' time and have the best of both worlds.

Makes 1 large loaf cake, takes around an hour, plus fruit-soaking time

YOU'LL NEED:

4 Earl Grey tea bags, for soakage

one of those 400g value bags of dried mixed fruit and peel

120ml light-coloured oil (sunflower or vegetable – not olive)

3 eggs

50ml milk (disnae matter if it's from a cow or not)

125g soft dark brown sugar[2]

250g self-raising flour, or plain flour with 2 teaspoons of baking powder added

½ teaspoon of ground cloves

a teaspoon of ground cinnamon

a pinch of salt

a grating of fresh nutmeg, or ½ teaspoon ground

OPTIONAL EXTRAS:

a splash of whisky or half a bottle of amaretto

zest of 1 big orange (optional, but highly pleasant)

2 tablespoons of golden syrup, honey, marmalade or apricot jam, for glazing

Make about 500ml of very strong Earl Grey tea using the tea bags and pour it into a bowl over the dried mixed fruit. You can add a dram or two here if you're into that, or alternatively skip the tea and glug over half a bottle of off-brand amaretto instead. Leave it to steep overnight, or while you're at work or writing your pesky dissertation research questions.

When you want to make the cake, preheat the oven to 170°C and line a large loaf tin with greaseproof paper or one of those handy liner things.

---

[1] You can also put this fruitcake in the bottom of a rucksack, which you will then inevitably leave on public transport because you're a chaotic little gnome. It'll be there when, three days later, you initiate a sheepish conversation with the lost-property woman who'll hand you your bag with a raised eyebrow she might lose a contact lens. Still tastes great, though.

[2] Fine, use plain white sugar if you don't have any brown, but add more cinnamon and a lick of treacle, if you too are from 1926.

Put all the remaining ingredients except the soaked fruit and the golden syrup into a large bowl and give them a good mix until properly combined. Drain the fruit[1] and add it in, mixing gently until evenly distributed. Slop the mixture into the cake tin and bake for around an hour, checking on it after 45 minutes. A skewer or fork prong inserted into the very middle should come out clean. If it's looking quite brown on the top but still gooey underneath, put some foil over it and pop it back in for 15 or so minutes.

When the cake comes out of the oven and is still warm, poke holes in it and brush it with some of the golden syrup or honey. This makes a nice sweet and soft crust after a few days. Alternatively, if you're not transporting this and have just made it because you're deathly bored or wanted to experiment with something other than hallucinogens, you can melt a little marmalade or apricot jam in the microwave and pour it over to make a nice sticky glaze.

This is brilliant thickly sliced and spread with butter, or you can just suck on the whole thing like you're teething again. Up to you.

[3] You can boil the excess here to make a syrup to brush over the cake if you don't want to use golden syrup.

VEGAN LEMON DRIZZLE CUPCAKES VG

When you look at the ingredient list, these feel like they shouldn't work – but good lord, I promise you they do. No one quite believes they're vegan, either, as they're so light and fluffy. These cakes are absolutely best on the day they're made, and have a tendency to go stale much faster than a lot of other cakes I've come across, but that's all the more reason to make them and eat them fresh, if you ask me. If you're feeling fancy, you can introduce a more sophisticated flavour by adding a few *very* finely chopped needles off a small sprig of rosemary to the batter, then infusing the syrup with the remainder. And if you don't have a 12-hole muffin pan or paper cases, then that's fine; this works in a well-greased 450g[1] loaf tin, too. Just up the cooking time by 5 minutes.

Makes 12, takes 45 minutes total

YOU'LL NEED:

For the cakes

270g plain flour

200g sugar, either caster or granulated

a heaped teaspoon of baking powder

a pinch of salt

100ml light oil, either vegetable or sunflower

150ml sparkling water (tap water works too; it just won't be as fluffy)

zest and juice of a small lemon

For the drizzle

2 more small lemons

2 tablespoons of granulated sugar, for sprinkling (I like them a little crunchy)

4–5 tablespoons of sugar

Preheat the oven to 180°C. Line a 12-hole muffin tray with 12 cupcake liners.

In a large bowl, combine the flour, sugar, baking powder and salt with the oil, water and lemon juice and zest. Because of the lemon juice and baking powder, the whole thing will fizz, but don't worry – this is normal. Spoon roughly 2 tablespoons of mix into each cupcake case, filling them around three-quarters full. Bake for 15–20 minutes (check them after 15) until pale golden and springy to the touch.

While the cakes are in the oven, zest both the remaining lemons and combine the zest in a bowl with 2 tablespoons of granulated sugar. Put this aside for sprinkling later.

In a small saucepan, combine the juice of both the lemons with 4–5 tablespoons of sugar, tasting as you go to determine if you'd prefer it more or less sweet. Bring this to a simmer, and as soon as it starts to bubble and look syrupy, turn off the heat.

While the cakes are still warm and in the tin, poke little holes in their tops, either with a toothpick, a skewer or the tip of a small knife. Using a teaspoon, drizzle a couple of teaspoons of the warm syrup over each cake, then top each one with a small pinch of the zesty sugar. Evenly distribute any remaining syrup over the cakes, but put the rest of the zesty sugar aside for a later date (it'll keep in one of those tiny airtight containers) and use on pancakes, or in a cheesecake base.

---

[1] As in, the tin shouldn't weigh 450g. That's the weight of the mix it's designed for, innit.

ALMOND, MAPLE AND TAHINI COOKIES (VG) (GF)

The middle of the Venn diagram of gluten-free and vegan bakes that don't use some sort of specialised flour or binding agent is quite sparsely populated. This is one of the few recipes that sits in this sacred space, utilising ground almonds and the brilliant nutty bitterness of tahini to make quite a grown-up tasting cookie. The original recipe is by Katarina Cermelj, and first appeared on the *Guardian*'s website in 2021, but I've changed it up here, substituting almond flour for cheaper and coarser ground almonds, omitting the sesame-seed coating, and adding a dash of almond extract alongside the vanilla. And yes, maple syrup is eye-wateringly expensive, so if you're watching the pennies, golden syrup works perfectly well here too – or if you're vegan't, honey is also excellent. It's important to either cook these on a silicone baking mat, if you have one, or use two or three layers of baking paper, as they have a tendency to burn on the bottom if you use cheap baking trays, as I do.

Makes 12–14, takes 45 minutes total

YOU'LL NEED:

100g tahini

100g ground almonds

100g maple syrup or golden syrup

a capful – 2ml or so – of almond extract (it's strong stuff, so you really don't need much)

½ teaspoon of vanilla extract

a tiny pinch of salt

Preheat the oven to 165°C and oil and line two baking sheets (or use one and work in batches).

Combine everything in a small bowl and scoop golf-ball-sized amounts of the resulting dough into your hands, rolling them into balls. Repeat and place these balls over the prepared baking sheets, giving them plenty of space, as they'll spread as they cook. Spread a smidge of vegetable oil on the bottom of a glass to stop them sticking, then use the glass to press each ball down until they're around 1cm thick. Chill in the fridge for 20 minutes, or pop in the freezer for 10.

Once chilled, bake for 10–12 minutes, or until the edges are looking golden. These are super soft when they come out of the oven, so don't move them at all until they've cooled completely.

These will keep in an airtight container for around 2–3 days before going squishy.

ALMOST-PIZZA-EXPRESS-WORTHY CHOCCY FUDGE CAKE Ⓥ DFO

If cakes could get knighthoods, this would be Sir Moistcrumb of Fudgeville. Creamy, moist, sweet, yet still relatively fluffy, it's about as close as I can get it to the chocolate fudge cake at Pizza Express: the gold standard in both chocolate cakes and chain-restaurant desserts. I can't claim full ownership of the recipe, of course – it's a mishmash of different ones I've played around with on the interwebs – but I've engineered it so it doesn't explicitly require buttermilk, espresso powder or expensive vanilla bean paste; three very specific ingredients that can be offputting to the novice baker. Happily, it all comes together in one bowl, and is pretty difficult to mess up. And don't worry if the batter looks incredibly thin in comparison to a sponge cake mix – it's meant to be like that, as it uses a completely different method to creaming. Once you try it, you won't go back to any other way of making chocolate cake.

Oh, and the icing slaps too. Bring this to a potluck as dessert and be worshipped as the Cake God forever.

Makes one large double-layer chocolate cake, takes around 2.5 hours including cooling and icing

YOU'LL NEED:

For the cake

2 teaspoons of lemon juice or white wine vinegar

250ml milk (plant milk works fine)

250g plain flour

400g sugar (either caster or granulated)

100g cocoa powder (make sure you use proper cocoa powder for baking, not hot chocolate powder)

2 teaspoons of baking powder

a teaspoon of bicarbonate of soda (use an extra teaspoon of baking powder if you don't have this handy)

a big pinch of salt

2 large eggs, or 3 small ones – around 130–135g

a tablespoon of cheap, syrupy vanilla extract, or 2 teaspoons of good stuff[1]

125ml light-coloured vegetable or sunflower oil

250ml hot instant coffee,[2] made with a teaspoon of granules (don't worry, it won't make the whole thing taste like coffee) – if you're posh and don't have granules, make a weak cafetiere

For the mascarpone buttercream icing

50g butter or vegan block

250g mascarpone cheese (use vegan cream cheese to keep it all dairy-free)

300g icing sugar

2 tablespoons of boiling water

40g cocoa powder

2 teaspoons of cheap vanilla extract, or one of the good stuff

a pinch of salt

dark chocolate curls, to finish

---

[1] You'll be able to tell which is which, because the cheaper stuff usually has glucose syrup and colouring in it, and costs well under £1 for a little plastic bottle. The expensive stuff comes in larger bottles, and is more like £6–8 per 100ml.

[2] Coffee and vanilla really help to bring out the chocolate flavour, and are essential as the cake uses vegetable oil rather than butter.

Preheat the oven to 170°C. Grease and line two round 23cm cake tins, or use a 25cm square roasting tray.

To start the cake mix, add the lemon juice or white wine vinegar to the milk and set it aside for 5 minutes to curdle.

In a really big bowl, combine the flour, sugar, cocoa powder, baking powder, bicarbonate of soda and salt. Add the curdled milk, along with the eggs, vanilla extract and oil. Give everything a good mix until properly combined. Then, pour in the coffee, gently stirring it into the batter to incorporate the liquid.

Pour the batter into the tins and give them a tap and a shake on the counter to bring any big air bubbles to the top. Pop them in the oven for 28 minutes, then pull them out to check if they're cooked all the way through. They should spring back when touched, and a skewer inserted into the centre should come back clean. If there are still crumbs on the skewer, or if your fingers leave imprints, put the tins back in for another 5 minutes and check again.

When you're happy the cakes are done, leave them to cool in the tins for 15 minutes, then flip them out onto a wire baking rack, or a clean grill rack if you don't have a specified cooling rack. Carefully peel off the greaseproof paper and let the cakes come to room temperature while you make your icing. If you used a square pan, wait until the cake is cool, then carefully cut it in half through its equator.

To make the icing, place the butter in a large bowl and beat it with a balloon whisk (or with electricity) until pale and fluffy. Then, add your mascarpone and beat again until it's creamy and combined with the butter. Next, add the icing sugar and combine gently at first, so you don't end up with a cloud of sugar dust that settles over everything. Add a couple of tablespoons of boiling water to

the cocoa powder to make a thin paste and drizzle this into the bowl, along with the vanilla extract and a pinch of salt. Now, beat everything together until properly chocolatey. You're looking for a spreadable consistency, so if it needs a splash of milk, add some now. Making icing, unlike baking proper, isn't an exact sport, so if you think it could do with some more cocoa or vanilla, go for it.

When the cakes are completely cool – actually, hang on. Let me repeat that in bold, italicised capitals: *WHEN THE CAKES ARE COMPLETELY COOL*, scoop around a third of the buttercream over one of them, and spread it evenly to the edges before plonking the other one on top. Spread another third of the buttercream evenly on the top cake, and then blob the rest around the sides before smoothing everything with a hot table knife (dip it in boiling water – don't microwave it or anything).

To make things really pretty, you can use a hot teaspoon to make a nice swirl radiating from the middle of the cake and then around the sides. Top the whole shebang with some chocolate shavings you've taken off the side of a bar of dark chocolate using a vegetable peeler.

Voilà. Eat your heart out, Pizza Express.

SLAPDASH BREAD VG

Let it be known that I am no bread expert, but I make this slapdash loaf roughly once a week for myself, because it's brilliant. It's absolutely my go-to when I have zillions of mouths to feed, so I'll make it to go with the Sicilian-style Aubergine Stew (page 129), or the Mediterranean Chicken Stew with Olives But Not Sun Cream (page 71), or to dip into the Roasted Butternut Squash, Peanut Butter and Chilli Soup (page 135). It's great, as I can quickly make up the first part in the morning, leave it to do its thing, and end up cooking it just before I start on dinner.

I'm going to quack on for a bit longer than usual in this recipe intro, because I think it's important to know that this bread uses a bit of an unusual method, and it needs a bit of spiel to explain it. So do bear with me.

The method for this loaf is sort of a halfway house between two more common methods of making bread. Those methods are the traditional all-in-one style, kneaded for ages to develop the gluten,[1] then left to prove twice over; and the more contemporary 'no-knead' method, which takes up to 24 hours to ferment and uses a cast-iron casserole dish to get a good crust. Straddling those two ways of doing things, this recipe uses a wetter, yeastier, starter dough than the traditional one to produce a higher-hydration loaf, but doesn't need nearly as long to ferment as bread made with the 'no-knead' method. It produces a sturdy crust with a soft, short-ish crumb[2] and a very good depth of flavour.

Bread can be a temperamental creature, so there is no one-size-fits-all method in terms of how long everything will take, either in terms of proving or cooking. Unlike the other recipes in this chapter, the method below is a guide only. It's important to pay attention to the visual cues here rather than just the timings.

And my apologies if that introduction sounded like gibberish to you. You can make this loaf even if you don't know which way round a crumb structure should face - the instructions below will tell you, in plain English, exactly what you're looking for at each stage in this rather magical process.

This makes a biggish loaf that lasts about 15 minutes in my household. Halve it if you want a wee one.

Makes 1 big loaf, take an hour and 20 minutes, plus at least 4 hours to prove (but the more you can manage, the better)

YOU'LL NEED:

700g flour[3]

2 × 7g sachets of fast-action dried yeast

a teaspoon of sugar or honey

approximately 500ml warm water – not too hot

25ml extra virgin olive oil

1½ teaspoons of fine table salt

Start by putting 550g of the flour into a large bowl with the instant yeast and sugar and stir evenly to combine. Then add enough of the water and the olive oil to give you a wet, mud-like dough, around

---

[1] Gluten is one of the proteins found in wheat, rye and barley. When activated, it forms long strands that make a sort of gel-like mesh that traps moisture and air, giving your bread a good chew, and a bouncy texture.

[2] The olive oil in the dough makes the whole loaf softer, which I prefer, because fat inhibits some of the gluten production. You can play around with the quantities of olive oil you use.

[3] I use plain flour without any ill effect, but if you have strong bread flour on hand, do use that.

the viscosity of hotel breakfast porridge. Don't feel pressured to use all the water.

Cover this mixture with either clingfilm or a damp tea towel and put it in a warmish place for at least 2½ hours, but preferably 3–4. What you're looking for when you come back to it is for the dough to have risen up the sides of the bowl, forming stringy bits around the edges, and for it to be very jiggly if you give it a gentle shake. The mix should also have visible holes in it; that's where the air is sleeping, so don't disturb it too much. All this, like any good night out, should be accompanied by a beery smell. Bear in mind that the longer you leave it for here, the better, so you can go out and do all your bits and bobs while Captain Yeasty McYeastFace does his thing in the boiler cupboard.

When you're happy with your yeast monster, remove him from the warm place and fold in the salt and enough of the rest of the flour to make the dough roughly workable (you might not need it all). You (k)needn't knead it expressly here, but incorporating the flour on the work surface is often easier than doing it in the bowl. Do this all with a clean pair of hands (preferably yours), by the way – that way you'll be able to feel where there are still flour pockets that need to be incorporated. The dough will be very sticky, but don't worry; it's meant to be like that. That said, if you find that it's not holding its shape at all and splurging across the work surface, then yes, it's probably too runny, so add some extra flour. When you've incorporated enough of the remaining flour to have the loaf hold its shape, wash, then re-flour your hands and shape the loaf into a flattened sphere (or *boule*, if you want to speak Bread) by tucking the edges under itself on a floured baking sheet. Sprinkle with a tiny bit more flour, then re-cover with the clingfilm and leave it to rise again in the warm place for at least another 1½ hours, or until it's looking very bloated.

When you want to bake your loaf, score the bread using a sharp knife to cut a cross shape two-thirds of the way into the loaf. This is important to enable the loaf to cook evenly all the way through. Now, take out the top shelf of your oven so you just have the middle and bottom shelves remaining. Preheat the oven to 220°C. Boil the kettle with about a litre of water in it, then pour this water into a small but deep-sided roasting tray and place it on the bottom shelf. This is to create steam to make the crust all nice and crunchy.

When the oven reaches temperature, pop the bread on the middle shelf (if your oven runs hot, and it's burning within the first 10 minutes, reduce the heat to 200°C. Set a timer for 35 minutes, and check on the loaf; I often slide the bread off the tray at this point and flip it upside down to get a nice brown bottom to match the top. The bread is cooked if it sounds hollow when you tap the bottom; depending on the oven I'm using, this cooking time can vary between 40 and 55 minutes, so keep checking back and use your common sense.

When it's done, it's important that you take it out and either prop it up on its side somewhere so the steam doesn't make the bottom soggy, or be normal and use a wire baking rack. I don't have a wire baking rack, so I usually just take the entire oven shelf out and leave it to vibe on the hob.

Everyone says that you should wait for bread to cool down completely before you cut it. I leave mine for about 10 minutes until it's no longer face-meltingly hot, then say bollocks to waiting and tear into it. This is to the detriment of its texture, I'm sure, but I'm eating hot bread covered in salted butter, which blocks out the annoying advice of people who know better.

• •

VARIATIONS

Instead of using water in the mix, use a leftover can of lager from the night before.

Work through some mixed seeds when you add the second quantity of flour to give an impression of rustic healthfulness.

Chop up a couple of handfuls of walnuts, and find the same amount of dried cranberries. Throw them into the loaf alongside the salt and second little bit of flour. This, toasted with honey and butter is cracking.

• •

FOCACCIA-ISH

Focaccia is having a bit of a moment on the socials as I write this, and rightly so. It's absolutely the best subtype of bread. To make a rough-and-ready sort-of version of it, double the quantity of olive oil in the dough above and then do everything in the above instructions, up to the point of shaping the loaf. When you get to here, instead of turning it into a boule, slap it into a large, very well (extra virgin) oiled roasting tray, stretching and pressing it into the corners. Then, using oiled fingers, make little dimples all over the surface. Cover with the clingfilm and leave it to rise again for about an hour. When you want to bake it, drizzle it with more olive oil and flaky sea salt, then whack it in at 230°C for around 25–30 minutes (it cooks a lot faster than the boule loaf). Serve with more olive oil and balsamic for dipping.

· ·

FOCACCIA VARIATIONS

Smush a couple of handfuls of whole black or green olives into the top of it before baking.

Sprinkle lots of rosemary fronds over the top before baking.

Slip it inside a pillowcase and use as a comfortable and delicious pillow even Lenny Henry would be proud to sleep on.

· ·

UN-TRICKY VIKKI SPONGE ⓥ

A rant about sponge cakes, a painstakingly detailed sponge cake recipe, and more suggestions for pimping the old Victoria sponge.

I am not a fussy eater. I will put anything and everything into my mouth at least once. I would like to think I'm not a snobby eater, either, merrily squeezing Primula cream cheese from the tube directly onto my tongue, and going after Party Rings like a convenience-store caveman chasing a pastel-glazed woolly mammoth. There is little I actively refuse to eat besides goat's cheese.[1] That's about it in terms of proper dislikes. However, I have a vendetta against one very particular foodstuff for a multitude of reasons, and that foodstuff is cheap shop-bought sponge cakes.

Jamaica ginger cake aside, cheap sponge cakes made with glucose syrup and vegetable oils are a very sad imitation of the real thing. Of course, there are high-quality sponge cakes you can buy, made with real butter and real eggs, but this is not my gripe. My gripe is with those slabs of madeira cake with the texture of foam-board insulation, or those godawful cupcakes that are made with air and sadness, and have a cloying dollop of vegetable fat and icing sugar on the top, masquerading as buttercream. The reason, I think, that these cakes make me so sad, is that making your own is around 6 million times better in terms of taste, and is easier and less time-consuming than you think. Instead of scrolling for half an hour (very easy to do), you could make a sponge cake in that time, and be proud and satisfied, rather than wanting to rip all your hair out at the follicles and never speak to another human again. Plus, a simple sponge uses four ingredients that you probably already have: butter, sugar, eggs and flour. In that order, too.

If you've never made a cake before, follow the ridiculously detailed steps below. It's fail-safe, I promise. Losing your sponge-cake virginity is way better than losing your actual virginity, so if you've never done it before, relax, put on some nice music and enjoy the process – it'll take all of 20 minutes to prep, and 20 minutes to bake. If you're a promiscuous master-baker already, there are some flavour combos at the end you can try.

Every sponge cake recipe I've ever come across uses pre-measured-out ingredients, but that's not the way I do things, or indeed how anyone does things, so here's *exactly* what I do to make well-risen, light-textured and buttery sponges every time, without the aid of a stand, hand or gland mixer.

---

[1] I would love to like goat's cheese, but I just don't. Yes, I've had lots of versions, in lots of dishes. I simply do not like the way it tastes, and will hear no more about it.

TO LOSE YOUR SPONGE-CAKE VIRGINITY AND MAKE A BASIC 20CM SPONGE IN PAINSTAKING DETAIL SO THAT NOTHING WILL EVER GO WRONG:

Preheat the oven to 180°C. Please make sure you do this. If you skip this step, the rest of the bloody recipe will be pointless. Making sure your oven is hot before the cake goes in is essential for a good rise.

Weigh **2 eggs** and write down the number if you need to. This number, which should be around 100–140g, depending on the size of your eggs, is the number you'll be using to determine the quantities of butter, sugar and flour. So, if you have 132g of eggs, you'll need 132g each of butter, sugar and flour. Everything is a 1:1:1:1 ratio. I told you this was science. If you don't have scales, see page 174 for what to do.

Weigh out the egg-number's worth of room-temperature **butter** into a mixing bowl. Here's the first place where people go wrong – they try to use cold butter. Either make sure your butter is lovely, squishy and soft at room temperature, or, if it's come straight from a cold holiday in the fridge, put it in the microwave for no more than 5–10 seconds, watching it like a hawk if there's any sign of melting. We do not want melted butter. No *merci*. Now, using a metal balloon whisk or an electric one (or a wooden spoon if you don't have one of those), beat the butter until it's a bit fluffy. This also serves the purpose of softening it a bit more, and introducing a tiny bit of air already.

Add the egg-quotient's worth of **caster sugar** to the butter. If granulated is all you have, that'll do, but it won't be quite as fine-textured. Now, beat the butter and the sugar together. The mixture will be clumpy and grainy at first, but will soon homogenise. Keep beating. Most recipes call for a 'light and fluffy' texture, but I've always found this

description unhelpful. You'll know it's right when the colour has lightened a bit and it has become more voluminous, with the sugar somewhat more dissolved in the butter.

You'll add the eggs next. Here's the next place where it all goes tits-up: we're in classic curdling territory. To avoid curdling, beat the eggs together in a separate bowl and add them in tiny little increments, giving the mixture a very good beating after each addition. This is the bit that takes the most time. And, if it does curdle, don't worry, because it's not the end of the world – you'll just have a marginally less airy cake. Just move on to the next step. Add a teaspoon of **vanilla extract** here, if you like.

Flour time, innit. If you've been using a whisk the whole time, now is the moment to switch to a wooden spoon. Very gently mix in an egg-quotient's worth of **self-raising flour**, scooping from under the mixture each time, until everything is homogeneous and there are no pockets of flour left. Careful, though; if you mix it too much here, you'll lose all that precious air you incorporated earlier, and your cake will be tough. If you don't have self-raising, plain flour followed by a teaspoon of baking powder will do the same job. No stress.

(Oh, and as a side note, you really don't need to sift the flour. It makes only a marginal difference in terms of lightness, and in exchange for the tortuous process of washing up a sieve, it's just not worth it.)

The texture of the cake batter at this point should be a soft dropping consistency – you can interpret that any way you like, but when you tap a spoonful of the mixture off the side of the bowl, it should drop off the spoon and splat straight back down.

You're now ready to line a cake tin. In all my years of baking – I'm 23 and made my first cake unaided age six – I have rarely bothered cutting out baking paper in a circle and using it to line a tin, unless it's for something very special. For most occasions, including birthdays (sorry, friends), I tear off a rectangle of greaseproof or baking paper, scrunch it up very tightly into a ball, and then reopen it out into a 20cm cake tin that has had a drop of **veg oil** poured into the base. I then lay out the paper and press it into the corners of the tin, smearing the oil around as I go. The kaleidoscope of creases you'll have achieved from scrunching it will make the paper sit nicely in the corners. You can now dollop the mixture into the tin, and spread it about a bit – but don't worry too much, as that will happen in the oven when the fat melts.

Bake your cake for at least 17 minutes, not opening the oven *at all* for this amount of time. If you open the oven, the cake might sink, and then all that effort you went to will be wasted. Ovens are unreliable beasts, so after this point, use your senses more than the kitchen timer. A cake this size should usually take no more than 25 minutes to cook through, but if your oven is particularly cool, it could take 30. What you're looking for is a Gordon Brown on top, a lovely smell wafting through the flat, and a springy texture when you press it. I actually do not own a single skewer for the 'it should come out clean' test, but if you stick a cocktail stick, nose swab or chopstick into the middle of the cake, it shouldn't have any crumbs or batter sticking to it when you lift it out.

Leave the cake to cool a little before taking it out of the tin. If you're adding icing, make sure it's completely cold before doing so. You can speed up this process by driving it up to Scotland in May and leaving it on an Edinburgh tenement windowsill for about 3 minutes.

I like this quick style of cake as it is, warm from the tin and maybe spread with a smear of jam. It honestly doesn't need much more than that, but this *is* the the sweet, puddingy end of the book, and so I have provided some exciting variations below if you're serving it for dessert.

THE NO SCALES METHOD

I have whipped up sponge cakes using this method when I've had nothing to measure with except hope and half a brain cell. It makes for a larger sponge, but usually I'm at someone else's house, and feeding other people anyway, so everything gets eaten. Basically, you follow the steps above, but you use a full American cup to measure the ingredients a 1:2:3:4 ratio. That's 1 cup of butter, 2 cups of sugar, 3 cups of flour and 4 eggs. If you don't have a standard cup measurement, find a measuring jug with millilitre calibrations and measure 234ml of water, then tip that into a mug, marking where the water line is with a Sharpie or something before tipping out the water. Once you've marked your 'cup' you can use the 1:2:3:4 ratio of ingredients as detailed above. And yes, this is convoluted, but it really shows the lengths I'll go to in order to have warm and fluffy homemade cake.

HOW TO TURN SPONGE CAKE INTO DESSERT

Your first option is to poke holes in the top while it's still warm, and pour into them some sort of syrup. This is the whole premise of a lemon drizzle cake. Squeeze the juice of 1 large **lemon** into a small saucepan and add 2–3 heaped tablespoons of white **sugar**, or enough so it no longer turns your face inside out. Heat it gently until the sugar dissolves, and then boil it until it's a bit thicker and bubbling nicely. Pour it over the cake while it's still in the tin, sprinkle with more sugar for crunch and serve warm with **clotted cream**. This also works with any other citrus fruit – and you can do it with coffee, too.

Secondly, you can serve this sponge cake with pillowy **whipped cream** and **mixed berries** from the freezer, defrosted quickly in the microwave or on the stove. Whip the cream with a tablespoon or so of **rum or whisky** and a dash of **icing sugar**. You can be fancy and spread it onto the cake, topping it with the berries, which should leak pleasingly into the cream. Or you can be lazy and simply put all the elements on the table and let people assemble for themselves what is basically a deconstructed Victoria sponge.

Another way to spruce up a sponge cake is by adding slices of fruit on the top before you bake it. This works brilliantly with apples. Chop an **apple** (any apple, it doesn't matter) into thin, hemispherical slices (I never bother peeling it, but you can if you like). Use the slices to top a sponge mix that has been introduced to a teaspoon of **cinnamon**, and is already sitting pretty in the tin. Push the apple slices into the mix vertically and close together. The cake batter should come up between the apple slices, like mud through your toes at a particularly fun festival. A great thing to do here is mix a little **granulated sugar** with more cinnamon and sprinkle it over the top before you bake it. It forms a crust that contrasts nicely with

the softness of the sponge and apples below it. You also might want to up the cooking time on this one, as the moisture from the apples can make the sponge bake more slowly. This is fantastic warm, with **toffee or honeycomb ice cream**.

A similar idea that mixes these two approaches is my invention of the plum, almond and orange blossom cake. Just after beating the eggs, add ½ teaspoon of **almond extract** and ½ teaspoon of **orange blossom water** to the cake mix. You can get both of these things cheaply at your local Middle Eastern store – don't bother with a supermarket, or you'll be ripped off. Push thin slices from 2 **plums** into the top of the uncooked cake mix, arranging them in a circular pattern if you want it to look pretty. While it's baking, add 50ml **water** and 2 heaped tablespoons of **sugar** to a pan, with a teaspoon of orange blossom water. Heat this until it's syrupy and bubbling, then pour over the warm cake when it comes out of the oven. You don't need anything with this; it's moist and rich enough as it is.

BONUS VERY RICH CUSTARD RECIPE

This is how I suggest you use up all the egg yolks left over from the pavlova on page 115. Mix all 8 **egg yolks** with 175g of **caster sugar** and 6 tablespoons of **cornflour**. Then heat 1 litre of **whole milk** in a saucepan with a 600ml tub of **double cream**, some **vanilla extract** and some ground **nutmeg**. When the milk is hot, pour it a little at a time into the egg yolk mix, whisking constantly. Return all that to the pan and whisk on a low heat until thickened.

Some ideas for using said custard: pour into an ice-cream maker if you have one, and make creamy vanilla ice cream; pour into ramekins and top with sugar before whacking under the grill for the ultimate crème brulée; dye it pink and cosplay Noo Noo from the *Teletubbies*, or simply drink the stuff until you can drink no more.

SHRUBBLE-TOOTING

If every dish you've ever cooked has turned out to be utter perfection, then you're either some sort of kitchen wizard, or lying. Like any other skill in life, a very natural part of cooking is to have the occasional mishap – maybe you took your eye off the ball for a minute and the toasted nuts under the grill are now baby lumps of charcoal, or perhaps the salt shaker's lid came off halfway through a little shake and now your soup tastes like someone boiled the Dead Sea and served it in Himalayan salt shot glasses. Most of the time, however, things won't be so catastrophic, and all you need to do is make some little adjustments to make it all better again. This section should cover how to identify a few common mistakes, and, most importantly, give you an idea of how to fix them.

COMPLAINT: MY FOOD TASTES BLAND, EVEN THOUGH I ADDED SALT AT THE END

Look, I know I bang on and on about it, but if your food tastes bland, you're probably not using salt correctly. Adding salt only at the end – or worse, at the table – is like going back over a mediocre essay and using the thesaurus function to change every other word to a longer one to make it appear cleverer. Sure, it might be a little better than doing nothing at all, but it'll still lack depth, and may come across as slightly tasteless.

Weaving enough salinity through your dish as you go is very important for both texture and flavour. It doesn't necessarily have to be table salt, either; anchovies, hard cheeses, soy sauce, bacon, Marmite, Worcestershire sauce, stock cubes, MSG and Parma ham are all fabulous sources of salt that bring their own character to your food. My advice, again, is to taste, then season lightly at *every stage* of cooking, from frying off onions to adding your tomatoes – before simmering, after simmering, and before serving. And always salt the water in which your carbohydrates, such as pasta and potatoes, are cooking. Doing all this seasons everything from the inside out, rather than making big adjustments at the last minute that might skew or hide something more delicate. You're at a bigger risk of oversalting if you do it last minute, especially as the saltiness will be 'on top', rather than permeating through all the layers of the dish.

COMPLAINT: BUGGER, MY FOOD IS WAY TOO SALTY

Right, so now you know the limit. Maybe you just weren't paying attention, or added table salt as well as stock and cheese, forgetting that those ingredients came with salinity of their own. Either way, your dish is too salty, and you need to rectify it. If it comes under 'slop' (as in, consists of something liquidy, such as stew, pasta sauces, soup, dal or curry), then this is actually quite easy to resolve. All you need to do is add enough unsalted ingredients to balance things out. For example, if it's a soup, you can add more water and make it thinner; you can blend in a couple of large potatoes you've cooked for 15 minutes in the microwave; you can add more vegetables, such as frozen peas, if that'll work in the flavour profile; you can add tins of chickpeas or butter beans to add thickness again after you've watered it down a bit. The same goes for all other slop: just add more stuff. It might still be a tiny bit salty, but if you've got rice, salad or some other carb with it, you'll get away with it. Just don't season anything else that's going with it, if you can help it.

That said, if you've really overdone it (and by that I mean, you've not got enough stuff in the cupboards left to balance out the whole thing), then tip half of it into a big Tupperware, and label it as 'extra salty soup/dal/stew/base'. Then, top up the rest with anything you do have on hand, noting down what you're adding so you can do the same in a few months' time with the frozen stuff. You might end up with a slightly different dish, but at least you won't have thrown any of it away.

As always with these things, prevention is better than cure. So go lightly at first, and build it up until you're happy with it. Don't shake the salt in, anyway – you'll never know how much you've added without tasting it. Instead, pinch it from a bigger dish, or pour it out into your hand or a teaspoon so you can eyeball exactly how much is going in each time. You'll soon get a feel for it.

For a much better explanation on how salt really works in your food, I cannot recommend Samin Nosrat's *Salt, Fat, Acid, Heat* highly enough. Do put it on the old wish list.

COMPLAINT: MY FOOD IS SEASONED WELL, BUT IT'S NOT GOT THAT CERTAIN *JE NE SAIS QUOIS*

I must make a confession here. Whenever I have instructed you to 'season' in this book, I've usually been devoting my energy to salt. But there is another type of seasoning that I've neglected slightly, and without wishing to chase the shadow of the great Samin Nosrat too much, that seasoning is acidity.

If your dish has enough salinity, then it could just be missing a touch of acid at the end. This could be a lick of vinegar, or a squeeze of lime juice; something, anyway, that will perk things up a bit. Ketchup, brown sauce, chutney, fresh tomatoes, cornichons, the gherkin in your Big Mac; these are all ways of introducing acidity, which balances out both the fat and salt of a dish. Hot sauce does the same thing – a primary ingredient in most hot sauces being vinegar – it just has a boatload of heat along with it. So, if your dish is lacking a little something, add a skoosh of lemon juice at the end; spoon a nice layer of sharp blackcurrant jam onto a bought vanilla cheesecake; perhaps

introduce a squirt of lime juice to the noods; pop some chopped-up pickled onions in your cheese toastie. It's a very fun game to play when you get the hang of it. By the way, you'll notice that most of these are last-minute additions. That's because acid slows down cooking a little, so only add it near-ish to the end.

COMPLAINT: THERE'S STILL SOMETHING MISSING

The other tools in your arsenal are bloomed spices (which are added near the beginning of the dish), chillies, lemon zest and fresh herbs. Use all of these things as you would shading in a drawing or painting: the main ingredients, plus the acid, salt and fat, form the overall structure of the piece, but the herbs, spices and chillies will add contrast and colour. As always, taste and adjust, and don't be afraid to use more than the recipe suggests.

COMPLAINT: MY VEGETABLES AREN'T GOING BROWN LIKE YOU SAID THEY WOULD

Pan's too full. Or too cold. Cook your stuff in smaller batches, and make sure to preheat your pan – and the fat in it – before anything else goes in. This applies mainly to things cooked on the stove, but the pan or tray being overcrowded can also cause problems in the oven. If in doubt, spread it over two baking trays.

COMPLAINT: EVERYTHING'S BURNING AND STICKING IN THE PAN

Turn down the heat first of all; you could even try taking the pan off the heat for a bit altogether. Go slowly, friend. Also, consider getting some pans that aren't made of tin foil – you know, the ones with a slightly heavier base. Extra oil or fat also evens up cooking on some occasions. By the way, if you're using non-stick, always use plastic or wooden utensils rather than metal ones to preserve the non-stickiness.

COMPLAINT: NO MATTER WHAT I DO, MY OVEN BURNS THINGS

Your oven probably runs too hot. So turn it down by 10°C or so, depending on what the recipe states, and reduce the cooking time by 5–10 minutes, too, checking on things as you go. I invested in an oven thermometer once, and it told me the oven in my student halls was running around 15°C hotter than it said it was. Then I tried to wash it one time (the thermometer, not the oven) and it broke, so I've used intuition ever since. Many nonnas will test the temperature of an oven by sticking their hand in it, and the more you cook, the more you'll get to know what feels right. An oven thermometer will help, though, and this is especially important if you're just starting out on the baking side of things.

COMPLAINT: MY SLOP IS TOO THICK

Add liquid – water, stock, wine, or even another tin of tomatoes will probably do the job.

COMPLAINT: MY SLOP IS TOO THIN

Cook it for longer, innit. If that doesn't work, add more stuff that'll soak up some of the water, such as potatoes, a blitzed tin of chickpeas or, on some

very specific occasions, small pasta shapes. Only very cautiously should you attempt to add flour, cornflour or a different thickening agent – if you do, make sure you mix it with a bit of water first, and then a little bit of the sauce on its own in a separate bowl. This is to ensure you don't have end up with any lumpage whatsoever. And cook out the flour very thoroughly so you don't have anything grainy going on. There is very much a risk of gloopiness in this scenario, so be careful with the amount you add.

COMPLAINT: MY MEAT IS TOO DRY

A lot of internet guides will say things like, 'Marinate your chicken breasts in yogurt to retain moisture,' or 'Soak your turkey overnight for the juiciest meat ever,' but in my experience, the best thing to do to keep meat from going dry is not bloody overcook it in the first place.

I grew up chewing through pork chops that had the same texture as a washed-up flip-flop, sawing through grey bits of topside on a Sunday, and eating fish that had turned to chalk dust after 40 minutes in the oven. Of course, no one wants to get ill, but there is a happy medium of 'deliciously moist but really still won't poison you'.

What you should do to reach moist blissfulness is cook your meat for the minimum recommended time in the recipe, then check the thickest part of it with a knife for visual, textural clues,[1] or use a meat thermometer to check for the correct temperature, which you'll have googled (disclaimer: I don't have one of those; I just use my eyes and have never been ill from uncooked meat).

[1] A cooked bit of chicken shouldn't have any pink bits, and the juices should run clear, not cloudy. The same goes for pork. I like my lamb legs and beef topside to blush heavily in the middle, but not be raw in the same way that I like the middle of my steak. That should come out still mooing.

Another way to even up cooking times is to tenderise or flatten bits of meat that have got an uneven texture. This is why if you cook a chicken breast whole (a very bad idea), you'll end up with a dry pointy bit and a pink middle. To cook a whole chicken breast evenly, cut it nearly in half, then open it out like a book. Then get out a big hammer or a wine bottle and flatten it to an even thickness (between two layers of clingfilm, so you don't get raw chicken splattered everywhere). The same thing goes for steak if it's unevenly butchered. And if you're really worried about meat giving you food poisoning, then just slow-cook tougher joints in a lot of liquid for 5–6 hours instead, or become a vegetarian. You really can't fail that way.

THE REAL SECRET TO MOIST MEAT

There is, however, something you can do to retain moisture in addition to not overcooking your meat, and it's called dry-brining. Dry-brining refers to the process of dusting your meat with a layer of salt, then leaving it to permeate the skin for A Long Time before cooking. It's a total game-changer if you've not tried it before, because not only does it result in moist, well-seasoned meat on the inside, you also end up with an amazingly crispy skin. This is to do with osmosis: the salt pulls the water out of the meat first of all, then it reabsorbs evenly, then you dry off the skin or surface and it crisps up.[2]

The longer you leave the salt on, the better, but even salting things half an hour before you're due to cook your chicken wings or drumsticks will make a huge difference to the texture, both inside and out. I'll dry-brine a whole chicken, or big joints of meat overnight in the fridge[3] – and just

to reassure you that it really works, I know a chef who would leave his steaks overnight in a big tray of salt. When it's time to cook everything, pat the surface dry with a bit of kitchen roll, add a tiny bit of oil or butter and the rest of your seasonings, and let the oven or pan work its magic. Honestly, it's such a revelation.

By the way, this doesn't work on fish or burgers, both of which should be salted at the very last minute before cooking, or they'll become tough. You also needn't bother with dry-brining for slow-cooked joints, as they're usually surrounded by a nicely seasoned braising liquid, which makes sure the muscle fibres don't dry out.

[2] For a more detailed explanation, read Sasha Marx's excellent post on the whole shebang at www.seriouseats.com/how-to-dry-brine. Or, again, read *Salt, Fat, Acid, Heat* (I swear I'm not part of a pyramid scheme).

[3] I have a friend who used to work the butcher counter at a supermarket, and would phone me whenever he had a good deal on, so I could toddle down – and he let me use his staff discount, too. He's a landscape gardener now, sadly, so my days of getting 2kg of prime beef forerib for £12 are over, which is very sad because there's no way I can buy that sort of thing at full price.

FURTHER READING

I could make a list the length of my arm when it comes to cookbooks I love, but I've chatted so much already that I'm running out of space, so here are the bare bones of what to read to improve your understanding of cooking and how it works. There are a couple of cookbooks 'proper' thrown in if you want some more dinspiration you don't have to think much about. And some YouTubers. Obviously.

SALT, FAT, ACID, HEAT by Samin Nosrat

A bible on how to improvise with food, which I've referenced throughout this book. It's a paving slab of a book, but Samin writes so beautifully, and it has some gorgeous illustrations, so getting through it shouldn't be too challenging.

THE FLAVOUR THESAURUS by Niki Segnit

A gem of a book to refer to when you want to know which ingredients go with what and why. It doesn't look anything like a cookbook, but it still has recipes, stories and lots of ideas for how to use up the ingredients in your fridge in unexpected ways.

SERIOUS EATS (SERIOUSEATS.COM)

A website devoted to unpacking the science behind home cooking in witty, engaging, evidence-based prose. Check out Kenji López-Alt's channel on YouTube too.

THE ROASTING TIN SERIES by Rukmini Iyer

Any one of these books is excellent for saving on washing up and doing things in a chilled, hands-off manner. Ingredients can be slightly on the pricey end, but *The Green Roasting Tin* (the veggie version) solves that one somewhat. The books are also *stunning* to look at.

NAT'S WHAT I RECKON

Go and watch everything Nat has ever produced on YouTube. He's my favourite food content person in the WORLD.

VITTLES SUBSTACK

If you've got a spare few quid a month, subscribe to Vittles for loads of brilliant deep-dives which explore culture, diaspora, identity and politics through food. It's London-heavy at the moment but that's slowly being rectified. Jonathan Nunn is a legend.

INDEX

W

V

ACKNOWLEDGMENTS

This book fell out of me. But only because I was hoiked upside-down by my ankles and then tickled by a variety of nice people until all the right words came tumbling out. This is where I'm going to thank them all, and everyone else involved in this process, for their superb efforts.

The first person to turn my world upside-down was the *Observer*'s Restaurant Critic, Jay Rayner. Not only did he share my blog (unprovoked) to his 330k followers on Twitter back in 2021, he also co-edited my first *Guardian* article, plonked some important links in front of the literary agency Lutyens & Rubinstein, then took me for lunch at Bentley's Oyster Bar and Grill. Oh, and subsequently recommended me as a panellist for BBC R4's *The Kitchen Cabinet*. He is therefore entitled to take all the credit for any success I ever have for the rest of my life. Cheers, Jay.

The next person to thank is my marvellous agent, Daisy Parente. She is the world's kindest, wisest, most encouraging person, and seems to know exactly what I want a long time before I do. Daisy did most of the tickling to make sure this book fell out in the right shape, with the right ideas in the right order. I'm so chuffed to be working with her.

Of course, this book wouldn't be in your hands without my brilliant editor Emily Brickell, who just *got it* from day one. Emily's attention to detail and organisation are second to none, and she always remains professional when telling me which of my ideas should never see the light of day and which made her snort coffee all over her monitor. She has been a dream to work with.

My next votes of thanks go to Libby Silbermann, who styled the food, and Luke Albert, who took the stunning photographs of it. They worked such magic on the shoot together, elevating each recipe to magnificent herb-speckled heights. Thanks go to assistants Florence and Sophie here, too.

And speaking of beautiful things, a big thank you goes to Steph, for her work on the book design. She also took all my *very* rough sketches for illustrations, and reimagined them so they looked a hundred times better. They really bring the book to life.

My next thank you is to the whole team at Ebury for their huge enthusiasm for *Do Yourself a Flavour*, and for being so supportive and informative with me on my first book. You're fabulously talented people and I've loved working with you all.

My penultimate thanks go to the bloody gannets I call friends. You lot have absolutely ruined my serving sizes, and made me a very lazy cook because you'll eat anything I put in front of you without comment, apart from 'can I have some more please?' Anyway, cheers for being behind me all the way, from reading the early days of my blog, to providing hilarious food-based anecdotes for me to write about. Special thanks go to Lewis, Amanda, Conor, Eve and Lucy, plus the rest of the EUMC crew – you know who you are.

And lastly, dear reader, I would like to thank you. Thank you for picking up this book, for getting to the end of it, and for cooking my recipes. It all means a lot to me, it really does, and while I don't think you can ever appreciate an acknowledgements section until you've written one yourself, do believe me when I say that you're the most important element in making this work. Promise.

ABOUT THE AUTHOR

Hiya. That's me on the page opposite, although I'm bigger in real life (but not by much). You've waited since the introduction to be nosy, so here's a bit more about me, as a delicious after-cookbook treat.

As a teenager, I was responsible for much of the family food shop and home cooking, and also had a number of kitchen jobs to keep me afloat. By the time I started uni, economising was old hat to me, but I soon realised that not everyone knew how to check price per 100g labels, or make a filling soup out of a few manky vegetables. I decided to start a blog to share that sort of knowledge with the friends I fed on a regular basis, rather than writing out the same recipe six times a fortnight when the inevitable requests came through. I learned that I rather liked writing, especially those introductions that everyone so loves to complain about on social media.

I kept the blog going over my time at uni (I have an English Language and Linguistics degree from the University of Edinburgh, if you're wondering, and no, they wouldn't let me write silly footnotes in my essays) but everything took off in my final year when a certain food critic with big hair and a jazz quartet tweeted my blog to the world. Suddenly, people were interested. And that, alongside a few other bits and bobs, is what has landed me here, trapped on the back page of this cookbook forever.

I jest. I am real. I have also written for several very real publications including the *Guardian* and the *Scotsman*, and my sultry southern British accent has probably wafted over your radio waves at some point as a panellist on BBC R4's *The Kitchen Cabinet*. When I'm not writing or thinking about food, I spend my time yeeting up and down the remote glens of northwest Scotland by mountain bike, touring skis, or on foot. Or buying hilarious tat in Glasgow's many charity shops.

If you want to speak to me in any capacity, Twitter's your best bet, but I've heard Instagram is the place to be these days so I'm also there, somewhat begrudgingly.

Tweet me: @FlissFreeborn
Gram me: @fliss_freeborn

flissfreeborn.com

1

Published in 2023 by Ebury Press an imprint of Ebury Publishing,
20 Vauxhall Bridge Road,
London SW1V 2SA

Ebury Press is part of the Penguin Random House group of companies
whose addresses can be found at global.penguinrandomhouse.com

First published by Ebury Press in 2023
www.penguin.co.uk

A CIP catalogue record for this book is available from the British Library

ISBN 9781529197242

Design by Stephanie Spartels at Studio Spartels
Photography by Luke Albert
Food and prop styling by Libby Silbermann
Copyedit by Tara O'Sullivan

Colour origination by Altaimage Ltd, London
Printed and bound in China by C&C Offset Printing Co., Ltd

Penguin Random House is committed to a sustainable future for our
business, our readers and our planet. This book is made from Forest
Stewardship Council. certified paper.